Blinded by the Lights

Blinded by the Lights

Texas High School Football and the Myth of Integration

Don E. Albrecht

TEXAS A&M UNIVERSITY PRESS
College Station

Library of Congress Cataloging-in-Publication Data

Names: Albrecht, Don E. author.
Title: Blinded by the lights: Texas high school football and the myth of
    integration / Don E. Albrecht.
Description: First edition. | College Station: Texas A&M University Press,
    [2025] | Series: Prairie View A&M University series | Includes
    bibliographical references and index.
Identifiers: LCCN 2024025614 (print) | LCCN 2024025615 (ebook) | ISBN
    9781648432750 (cloth) | ISBN 9781648432767 (ebook)
Subjects: LCSH: School sports—Social aspects—Texas. | Football—Social
    Aspects—Texas. | School integration—Texas—History. | De facto school
    Segregation—Texas. | Educational equalization—Texas. | BISAC: SPORTS &
    RECREATION / Cultural & Social Aspects | EDUCATION / Educational Policy
    & Reform / General
Classification: LCC GV584.T4 A53 2025 (print) | LCC GV584.T4 (ebook) |
    DDC 796.332/62089009764—dc23/eng/20240715
LC record available at https://lccn.loc.gov/2024025614
LC ebook record available at https://lccn.loc.gov/2024025615

Contents

Series Editor's Foreword

Ronald E. Goodwin, Prairie View A&M University

In May 1954, in a unanimous decision, the US Supreme Court over-turned its previous ruling in Plessy v. Ferguson (1896). In doing so, the court effectively ended segregation in public education and the societal policy of "separate but equal." Those in the Black community who grew up during this era knew that those separate Black schools were seldom, if ever, equal to their White counterparts. Even with secondhand books and other "hand-me-down" educational materials, those dedicated Black teachers gave their students the building blocks of education while preparing them for life in a society that continued minimizing their God-given abilities. Sadly, in many communities across this country, full integration of K–12 schools did not occur until the 1970s.

As a southern state, racism in Texas was similar to that found in other former Confederate states: White supremacists used violence and the rule of law to keep the Black community mired in substandard housing and low-paying jobs while offering an inferior education that systemat-ically denied them the same opportunities afforded to their European neighbors. There are numerous examples of Jim Crow-inspired violence throughout Texas' history. From Jesse Washington to James Byrd, the Black community was routinely reminded that race was the preeminent determinant in evaluating future societal and economic success.

Still, behind the veil of Jim Crow was a vibrant and close-knit Black community—a community that celebrated its accomplishments and dreamed of a future where race would not be a scarlet letter of shame. Some of those accomplishments occurred on the high school football fields across Texas. After the *Brown v. Board of Education* decision in 1954, many talented Black athletes starred on their high school and college football teams. Most, like Bubba Smith and Joe Greene, would have been restricted to segregated high schools in the Prairie View Interscholastic League (the segregated counterpart to the University Interscholastic League, which governs high school athletics in Texas) or one of the state's historically Black colleges and universities before 1970. But their successes as athletes proved that God-given talents were not only bestowed upon White children.

For example, God blessed Earl Campbell with unique physical gifts. Those gifts allowed him to routinely electrify the University of Texas' home crowd at the Darrell Royal-Texas Memorial Stadium on his way to a Heisman Trophy in 1977. Likewise, Eric Dickerson was also blessed. He had the speed and tenacity of a gazelle and powered Southern Methodist University's legendary Pony Express with Craig James in the early 1980s. While the mostly White home crowds at UT and SMU cheered the success of these teams, most would probably bristle at the thought of either the Campbell or Dickerson families living in their neighborhoods.

The intersection of race and sports is a well-trod avenue. But there is something different about Don Albrecht's *Blinded by the Lights: Texas High School Football and the Myth of Integration* that definitely adds to the conversation. He examines Texas' high school football and the impact of racial segregation, then integration, and then what he refers to as "resegregation." Even though the Supreme Court demanded schools integrate (albeit without a specific time frame), middle-class Whites chose to maintain all-White schools through the development of suburban school districts beginning in the 1970s. Today, while segregation is no longer the law, Albrecht notes schools are just as segregated as they were in the 1950s.

The reader will be drawn to Albrecht's stories of Black high school football players and their struggles for acceptance and recognition. But it is his analysis of Texas' complex racial problems that will leave the most lasting impression. Race is not merely a discussion or analysis of one's skin color. It involves the advantages, or disadvantages, of where one lives, the economic realities of a too-often ineffective education system, and the challenges inherent in single-parent households. Albrecht found that these and other influences eroded the initial promises of the *Brown* decision, as he believes racial progress is no longer evolving but instead regressing. Even though he doesn't seek to remedy the problems found in Texas' low-income schools today, he wants the reader to understand the realities facing those communities, too many of which are dispropor-tionately Black and brown.

The reader will find Albrecht's prose entertaining and with just enough academic-speak as evidence of his intense research skills. The author also admits that this manuscript "took thirty years to complete." I'm thankful he had the patience and support to bring this story into our public consciousness. We will be better for it.

Acknowledgments

It took thirty years to complete this book. Many people were vital in the process, and I am deeply indebted to these individuals. Most critically, of course, are the scores of people I interviewed, both in the 1990s and in the 2020s. Everyone was gracious and transparent, and their insights were profound. I am convinced that the stories these people shared with me should never be forgotten.

My family was supportive and encouraging throughout this project. My family makes my life astounding and magical. My wife, Carol, has been by my side for a wonderful half century. Much of who I am and what I have accomplished is because of her. She is an insightful sociologist, and much of my understanding of inequality and human behavior comes from discussions with her. She has read much of what is written here and provided tremendous help.

This book would have never been completed without the help and encouragement of my son Mathew Albrecht. When he was younger, I would tell him the stories shared with me by the people I interviewed during the 1990s. Occasionally over the years, he would ask me when I was going to finish that book. As I began working on the book again in recent years, Mathew carefully read each chapter. He read some parts of the book several times. He made astute editorial suggestions.

My hope is this book will help open people's eyes to the millions of low-income minority children who are attending schools that are at least as bad as their ancestors attended prior to desegregation.

Blinded by the Lights

Prologue

One spring afternoon in the late 1980s, I was returning to my office from a class I was teaching at Texas A&M University when I decided to stop by Kyle Field to watch a few minutes of Aggie spring football practice. Nowadays, practices are closed, but at that time anyone could just walk in and watch whenever they wished. Texas A&M in the 1980s was shaped by its history as the state's land grant college, with much of the student body coming from small- and medium-sized towns throughout the state. Minority students were few and far between on campus. However, R. C. Slocum—the defensive coordinator who would later become head coach—had constructed the feared Wrecking Crew defenses that dominated the Southwest Conference from the mid-1980s through the mid-1990s by recruiting athletes from predominately Black inner-city high schools in Dallas and Houston, such as Carter, Kimball, and Yates.

I walked into the nearly empty Kyle Field, then a seventy-two thousand seat stadium with a gray concrete exterior and three towering decks of concrete bleachers that literally cast a shadow over much of the campus. I chose a seat near the sideline on the west side of the stadium, in the shade of the afternoon sun. I sat next to a middle-aged Black man with a trim mustache and the muscular build of a former linebacker. During our conversation, I learned that he was an assistant football coach at a predominately Black high school in South Dallas. He was watching the Aggies practice to get ideas to help his team. As we visited, our discussion turned to his days as a high school student and football player in the segregated Texas school system. I was enthralled as he talked about the Wednesday or Thursday night football games in the old Prairie View Interscholastic League (PVIL). He spoke proudly of the talented teams and coaches, and of the quality of football they played. He went on to talk about how even the most talented players at the Black schools were totally ignored by the major college football programs in Texas and

1

throughout the South. After completing high school, this man had gone on to play football at the all-Black Prairie View A&M University in the early 1960s. With their pick of the most talented Black players, Prairie View, Grambling, and other Black colleges in the South were fielding teams that played far from the spotlight but with talent that matched the national powerhouse programs of the day.

As I thought about this conversation over the next couple of years, the idea for this book emerged. After delving into the library (remember, this was pre-internet), I found surprisingly little had been written about the integration of Texas football. I spent many hours in the library finding articles and looking at microfiche copies of old Texas newspapers. The stories I read both enthralled and repulsed me. I began asking questions to anyone who would listen and to people who might have knowledge or information on the topic. At the time, I was fortunate to be teaching a class on the sociology of sports at Texas A&M, and I was helping the Aggie football team with their recruiting efforts. As a result, I was in contact with many people who were very knowledgeable about Texas football.

I began writing this book in the early 1990s. Over a period of a few years, I put together a significant share of an early draft. I interviewed scores of people, many of whom are mentioned by name in this book. I was most fortunate to have conducted these interviews when I did because many of these people have since died. Nearly everyone was extremely cooperative, and some went to the extra effort of sending newspaper clips to me or suggesting other people that I might talk to. Paul Register, Bubba Bean, Hugh McElroy, and Sammy Williams read drafts of my early manuscript.

Then, two situations emerged that prevented me from completing the book at that time. First, my research and writing at Texas A&M were on different issues, and demands from my growing family kept me so busy that I failed to find time to work on this project. Second, in many ways the 1990s were a time of optimism. The Cold War had just ended, and to me it seemed that we were entering a time of long-term peace and prosperity. While race relations in the United States were far from ideal, it seemed that we were moving in the right direction. Without question, race relations were far better in the 1990s than they had been in the 1950s and 1960s. Many people, including me, assumed progress would continue. The consequence was that Americans were more interested in celebrating that progress than looking back at the horrors of segregation and the painful process of desegregation in the still recent past. There was little interest in analyzing the problems that endured. Because of this, the draft of my book and my notes sat in my filing cabinet gathering dust for thirty years.

I am convinced that now is the time to blow the dust off my early draft, make the necessary updates, and tell important stories that should never be forgotten. As I read my notes and draft chapters, I was again startled by the way people were treated in this country during my life-time. The courage of the people whose stories are told in these pages filled me with hope for the future. So, I committed to finishing this book. Circumstances are now very different than they were thirty years ago—for me and for society. Personally, my time is no longer an issue. My pending retirement and my quiet life at home with my wife as an empty-nest couple means that I have plenty of time to think and write. Even more important, I am no longer convinced that our country is making progress down the long road to school desegregation and racial equality. Data clearly shows that elementary and high schools in Texas and elsewhere are significantly more segregated now than they were in the 1990s or even the 1970s. That is, the percentage of Black and Latino kids attending predominately minority schools that have high poverty levels is greater now than in 1990. Further, in many ways the predominately minority, low-income schools of today are in worse shape than the segregated schools of the 1950s and 1960s. A major reason for this is that the middle- and working-class individuals who held the minority community together and served as role models for neighbor-hood children have departed for suburbs that are wealthier, safer, and have better schools. Prior to desegregation, redlining and other policies meant that nearly all Black residents, regardless of wealth or education, were forced to live in the same neighborhoods in cities throughout the country. Additionally, many policies that were intended to protect racial minorities—and especially to ensure that they have a chance for a quality education in a quality school—have been stripped of their effectiveness.[1]

The average wealth of Black households is 900 percent less than that of White households, and the size of the gap, which narrowed from the 1950s through the 1990s, has ceased to close and is now widening.[2] An astounding one in three Black American men are incarcerated at some point in their lifetimes, a rate much higher than for White Americans.[3] Further, a glance at the news reveals numerous cases of blatant racism, including racially motivated violence and the growth of White supremacist groups. Dr. Ramona Houston from Brownwood, Texas, described how members of her family—educated, middle-class professionals—are regularly stopped by the police and at times have had guns pointed at their heads.[4] I interviewed Dr. Houston in 2023. I was fortunate to have interviewed her father in the 1990s. Her father, Cecil Houston, was a pioneering Black athlete at Brownwood High in the 1960s. Perhaps this book, by helping us remember our past, can allow us to understand the present and chart the way forward.

A large share of this book focuses on very talented and well-known Texas high school football players. Their stories provide a lens to observe what happened during the racial integration of Texas schools and in the decades since. Sports, in many ways, are a microcosm of society. Of course, most people who attend high school don't play football, and the vast majority of high school football players don't get a scholarship to play in college or go on to play professionally. In addition to the people talked about in this book, thousands of other people have lived through segregation, desegregation, and the resegregation processes, and many of their stories are as dramatic as those told here. My objective is simply to use football as a vehicle to tell a critically important story.

This book deploys the mirror that is Texas high school football to provide a novel view of changes in the broader society. The world of sports can often serve this role. In fact, some of the major battles in the war for racial equality have been waged in the sports arena, and sports played a prominent role in the battle for integration in this country. Both the competitive and cooperative aspects of sports can force participants and observers to accept each other as equals. In doing so, they are more likely to accept each other as equals in other areas of life. By looking at where we have come from and where we are in sports, a greater understanding of race relations in this country can be achieved.

This book focuses primarily on Texas high school football during the years since the end of World War II. However, it will be necessary to briefly describe some events that occurred prior to 1945 to better understand the historical context of the time. Texas does not exist in a vacuum, and many events that occurred outside of the state had major influences on race relations in Texas. In addition, many important events that influenced race relations in sports took place in the courtroom, on the city street, or in other places far removed from the sports arena. It is necessary that some of these events be briefly mentioned to provide context for this story.

Another relevant question is, "Why Texas high school football?" The topic of racial integration is huge, but focusing on one sport in one state results is a more manageable undertaking. Further, in many ways Texas is a microcosm of the rest of the country. Texas is a southern state, and the eastern part of the state has historically had demographics and culture similar to its neighbors to the east that comprise the Deep South. Race-based slavery was practiced throughout the state, and Texas fought with the South during the Civil War. Jim Crow laws were as ubiquitous and as strictly enforced in Texas as anywhere, and Texas has had its share of racially motivated beatings and lynch mobs. Often, integration efforts in Texas were as painful as they were in Mississippi or Alabama.

Yet, Texas is also very different in some ways from its southern neighbors. The huge state covers several climatic regions, and this climatic diversity has resulted in several social regions as well. In the eastern part of the state, slavery-based plantation agriculture was widespread, and today the racial composition of the population is similar to that of Louisiana, Arkansas, or Mississippi. In contrast, Hispanics are a majority in many South Texas counties. In parts of the plains of West Texas, the racial make-up of the population resembles Kansas or Nebraska. In these areas with much smaller Black populations, segregation was practiced, but it was not as much of a fundamental part of the social order.

While this book includes stories from across the state, it emphasizes five communities that show the diversity of experiences across the state. These five communities include the state's two largest cities (Houston and Dallas), the East Texas city of Beaumont, the medium-sized West Texas city of Odessa, and the smaller West Texas city of Brownwood. This story begins with a chapter providing the essential background to the story of the integration of Texas football. This includes a discussion of how a segregated society emerged and some of the early breakthroughs, from the courtrooms to the ballparks and stadiums, that led to ending this brutal system of separation.

Turning my thirty-year-old draft and notes into this book required me to retrace the steps that I followed in the 1990s. In recent months, I have interviewed numerous additional people who have insights on high school football, integration, and the changes occurring in recent decades. I have also spent countless hours reading books and articles on the topic. Again, I appreciate the insights provided by these people. Certainly, this book tells only a small fraction of the events that occurred in the integration of Texas schools. I would be very appreciative if anyone with additional experiences would contact me and share their stories. I would love to hear them.

Chapter One

Segregation

In 1776, Thomas Jefferson, a man who owned over a hundred slaves, penned the words, "all men are created equal" as part of the monumental Declaration of Independence. At US independence, slavery was legal in every state, and enslaved people accounted for about a fifth of the population of the new nation. As a political compromise, slaves counted as three-fifths of a person when determining political representation in Congress. During the decades immediately following the American Revolution, slavery was gradually abolished in all northern states, which were less economically reliant on the institution. Slavery, however, became only more firmly entrenched in southern states with the growth of "King Cotton."

Closely associated with the establishment of the American version of race-based slavery was the development of an ideology with corresponding values and norms that supported and justified slavery in the eyes of slaveholders and others. A basic part of this ideology was the contention of Black inferiority and White supremacy, which provided justification to some for the inhumane treatment that accompanied slavery. Numerous books were written, and pseudo-science employed, to convince the American people of the inferiority of the Black race.[1] Supreme Court Justice Roger Taney in *Dred Scott v. Sandford* (1857) stated that people of African descent were not and could never be citizens of the United States. As such, they had "no rights which the white man was bound to respect."

As a result of these efforts, the philosophy of Black inferiority became firmly entrenched in the minds of many Americans. Well over a century after the Dred Scott decision, NFL Hall of Fame football player Eric Dickerson from Sealy, Texas stated, "I grew up in the segregated South where the idea that Black people were inferior to White people was in the air we breathed."[2] As evidence of how thoroughly the notion of Black inferiority was ingrained, I regularly had people ask me if the Black students in my college classes could "keep up."

When the Mexican government invited White American settlers to enter Texas in the 1820s, many came from southern states. These early settlers not only brought their slaves with them, but the associated attitudes and institutions. Slavery was permitted in the Republic of Texas after it achieved independence from Mexico in 1836, and when Texas entered the United States as the twenty-eighth state in 1845, it was as a slave state. Texas joined its southern neighbors in seceding from the Union during the Civil War. The 1860 census, taken just prior to the Civil War, found that over 30 percent of the more than six hundred thousand residents of Texas were enslaved people.

In the midst of the Civil War, on January 1, 1863, President Abraham Lincoln issued the Emancipation Proclamation, which declared that slaves living in the states that were rebelling against the Union were free. Following the conclusion of the war, the Thirteenth, Fourteenth, and Fifteenth amendments of the Constitution were ratified. These amendments abolished slavery and badges of servitude, and they granted Black people all the rights and privileges enjoyed by every other American— including citizenship, equal protection under the law, and the right to vote.

During the Reconstruction years immediately following the Civil War, federal agents and troops were sent to the South partly to assure that Blacks were not denied their recently granted constitutional rights. Some of the achievements made during Reconstruction were impressive. In many parts of the South, Blacks represented a numerical majority of the population, which resulted in many Black persons and those sympathetic to their cause being elected to local, state, and even federal offices.[3] There was strong opposition to increased Black power from the historic power base of the South. The Ku Klux Klan emerged to use terror to prevent Blacks from utilizing their newly gained freedoms and political power. In some cases, riots and massacres occurred as White people sought to reestablish control. For example, on April 13, 1873, an estimated 150 Black people were killed in Colfax, Louisiana, by a White mob that included members of the KKK to prevent the loss of White power following the election of 1872.

In 1877, a political compromise was reached where Republicans agreed to end Reconstruction and withdraw federal troops from the South in exchange for Democrats accepting that Republican candidate Rutherford B. Hayes was the winner of the 1876 presidential election. In the years immediately following the end of Reconstruction, Black people continued to vote in large numbers and often held public office. During and shortly after reconstruction, twenty-two Black people were elected to the US House of Representatives from southern states, and two Black Senators (both from Mississippi) were elected.[4]

In the late 1880s and 1890s with Reconstruction ended, a series of political and economic events led to the erosion of conditions for Black Americans, especially in the South. By the end of the century, White supremacy reigned unchallenged in the South, impacting every aspect of life. Since the Constitution prevented explicit race-based voting bans, southern officials designed literacy tests, poll taxes, White primaries, and other tactics that effectively eliminated the Black vote. For example, in 1896 there were more than 130,000 registered Black voters in Louisiana; by 1904 there were only 1,342. In 1896, Black registered voters comprised a majority in twenty-six Louisiana parishes; in 1900 they comprised a majority in none.[5]

Speaking of the right to vote, President Lyndon Johnson stated:

> Every device of which human ingenuity is capable has been used to deny this right. The Negro citizen may go to register only to be told that the day is wrong, or the hour is late, or the official in charge is absent. And if he persists and if he manages to present himself to the registrar, he may be disqualified because he did not spell out his middle name or because he abbreviated a word on the application. And if he manages to fill out an application, he is given a test. The registrar is the sole judge of whether he passes the test. He may be asked to recite the entire constitution or explain the most complex provisions of state law. And even a college degree cannot be used to prove that he can read and write. For the fact is that the only way to pass these barriers is to show a white skin.[6]

Without the vote and the subsequent lack of power, Blacks were forced to accept menial jobs and denied educational opportunities. Around the turn of the century, a host of Jim Crow laws were approved throughout the South. These laws forbade Whites and Blacks from attending the same schools, riding in the same sections of trains and buses, receiving treatment in the same hospitals, or competing in the same athletic contests. Customs of the time required an even further separation of the races through the provision of separate toilets, water fountains, entrances, and exits. When Black people attended athletic events, they were forced to enter by a separate entrance and sit in a roped off Jim Crow section.[7] White businesses were generally happy to sell their goods and services to Black customers, but with restrictions. Black people could buy clothes but were not allowed to try them on; Black people could attend movies, but they had to sit in the balcony; Black people could get food from the restaurant but had to get take-out at the back door. In the extreme case, some small towns, known as "sundown" towns, completely excluded Black residents with threats of violence. There were hundreds of these towns throughout the South, including many in Texas.

Blacks who challenged racial conventions jeopardized not only their meager incomes but their lives as well. During the early decades of the twentieth century, mobs lynched scores of Black people each year, and the threat of physical reprisals were a vivid reality. During these years, there were more than three thousand Black people lynched in southern states; in Texas there were 468 documented lynching victims. Perhaps the most common accusation in southern lynching cases was that a Black man had raped or attempted to rape a White woman. It was dangerous for a Black man to violate, even slightly, carefully prescribed constraints on how he could interact with a white woman. In 1955, fourteen-year-old Emmett Till was murdered in Mississippi because he had reportedly flirted with a White woman. Eric Dickerson was taught by his mother, "There are two things that don't last long in this world; dogs that chase cars and Black boys that chase White girls."[8] No question, keeping Black boys away from White girls was a primary motivating factor in the development of a segregated school system. To provide one lynching example of the many that could be given, Bill Roan was killed by a mob on June 18, 1930, in Bryan, Texas, after a White woman claimed that he had attempted to rape her. The mob tracked Mr. Roan down and shot him. There was no arrest and no trial. No one was ever held responsible for Roan's death. This story is memorable to me because my family and I lived in Bryan for nearly thirty years.

Texas also experienced race massacres. Perhaps the worst was in Slocum, a small East Texas town in Anderson County near Palestine, on July 29–30, 1910. Causes of the massacre are uncertain. Some claim there were rumors of a Black uprising; others believe it was White anger after a Black boxer (Jack Johnson) defeated a previously unbeaten White boxer (James Jeffries) in what was billed as the fight of the century on July 4, 1910. During the massacre, armed White men moved through the Black section of town shooting every Black person they could find. Perhaps one hundred Black people were killed. Massacre suspects remained free throughout their lives.

The published literature from that era provides some indication of racial views of the day.[9] The *Atlantic Monthly* published a series of articles on "The Universal Supremacy of the Anglo-Saxon." Best-selling books included Charles Carroll's *The Negro: A Beast*, published in 1900, and Robert W. Shufeldt's *The Negro: A Menace to American Civilization*, published in 1906. Thomas Dixon's *The Clansman: A Historical Romance of the Ku Klux Klan* was published in 1905, and ten years later it was made into a feature film titled *The Birth of a Nation*. This film was such a success that it established Hollywood as the heart of the motion picture industry.

In 1895, while speaking before the Cotton Exposition in Atlanta, Booker T. Washington stated that the separation of the races was preferred by both, and he urged Black people to be happy with their place in life and try to improve themselves in their present situation. Black people should emphasize becoming better farmers, better mechanics, or be better at whatever they were doing. He also made it clear that he thought agitation by Blacks would be unwise and unproductive. Because these views were so popular among White people, they were readily accepted and strongly encouraged.

The separation of the races also received support from the federal government and several key court decisions. Of special significance, in 1896 the Supreme Court, by a vote of 8–1, gave constitutional sanction to governmentally imposed racial segregation. In *Plessy v. Ferguson*, the court endorsed the view that racial segregation did not constitute discrimination and that states by law could require the separation of races in public places as long as equal accommodations were provided for all. Of course in reality, separate but equal is virtually impossible to achieve and certainly seldom if ever occurred in the Jim Crow South.

Thus, when the twentieth century began, the separation of the races was virtually complete in Texas and the rest of the South. Many White persons would seldom interact with Black people except when acting in carefully prescribed caste roles. Segregation also resulted in extreme economic hardship for most Black people. Writing in the 1940s, Swedish economist and sociologist Gunnar Myrdal stated:

> The economic situation of the Negroes in America is pathological. Except for a small minority enjoying upper- or middle-class status, the masses of American Negro, in the rural South and in the seg-regated slum quarters in Southern cities, are destitute. They own little property; even their household goods are mostly inadequate and dilapidated. Their incomes are not only low but irregular. They thus live from day to day and have scant security for the future.[10]

In 1940, the income of the average Black family was only 41.1 percent as high as for the average White family. At that time, only 7.2 percent of adult Black men had a high school degree, and only 1.2 percent had a college degree.[11] Thus, during the first half of the twentieth century, Blacks living in Texas and elsewhere in the South had seen only marginal improvement in their living conditions since the end of slavery. For the most part, their lives provided little economic security and few opportunities to improve their lot. Largely isolated and ignored, residents of segregated Black neighborhoods created institutions, such as churches and schools, that helped their communities thrive. In time, vibrant but poverty-stricken Black communities developed in rural areas and in cities throughout Texas and the rest of the country. Talented and capable leaders emerged to lead these communities and institutions.

In the North, different forms of segregation and inequality were also firmly entrenched. In place of Jim Crow laws, residential "redlining" forced Black people into segregated and crowded neighborhoods. This tended to result in de facto school segregation. Wages in northern factories, however, were much better than southern fields, and in time the trickle of southern Blacks moving to northern industrial cities turned into a torrent.[12] This exodus was enhanced when the tractor, the mechanical cotton picker, and other technological developments in agriculture reduced the need for Black labor on southern farms, and many rural Black tenant families were simply evicted from their homes and land. Many families not moving north moved to southern cities such as Dallas and Houston where there were more and better paying jobs and other opportunities.

Segregation and Sports

On December 29, 1945, nearly forty-six thousand football fans had crowded into the Cotton Bowl in Dallas, Texas, which at the time had a listed seating capacity of forty-five thousand. The capacity crowd was not there to witness Texas, SMU, Oklahoma, or any of the other college football powers of the day. Rather, they had gathered to watch a couple of high school football teams battle for the Texas state football championship. The game had originally been scheduled for Ownby Stadium on the SMU campus but had been moved to the larger Cotton Bowl because of the tremendous demand for tickets. This particular championship game featured Waco High versus Highland Park High. Waco High was led by James "Froggie" Williams, who would later become an all-American at Rice University. Although two of Highland Park's best-known athletes (future NFL Hall of Famers Doak Walker and Bobby Layne) had recently graduated, the team still had a multitude of talented players. On this afternoon, the capacity crowd was treated to an evenly matched, hard-hitting defensive struggle. The game ended in a 7–7 tie after Waco missed a field goal late in the fourth quarter. The following day, the headlines on the front page of the *Dallas Morning News* described the game. The front page also included a huge aerial photograph of a packed Cotton Bowl stadium.[13]

A few days later, the Cotton Bowl was again filled to capacity. This time the occasion was the tenth Cotton Bowl Classic featuring the University of Texas, champions of the Southwest Conference, against the University of Missouri. In a game featuring a noticeable lack of defense,

Texas outscored Missouri 40–27. Former Highland Park High student
Bobby Layne was the star for the Longhorns, as he had a hand in every
Texas score.[14]

Looking back at these two games in the Cotton Bowl from the perspective of the present, the size of the crowds and the amount of media
coverage show that football has long been important to Texans. But
perhaps the most striking feature of these games is that every member
of all four teams was White. At the time, however, the segregation of
high school and college football in Texas was universal and formally
enshrined in state laws that required the strict separation of races in
public institutions such as Waco High, Highland Park High, and the
University of Texas. The Gilmer-Aiken Law of 1949 updated earlier segregation laws, and in part stated, "Separate schools shall be provided for
white and colored children." At that time, every single player in Major
League Baseball (MLB), the National Football League (NFL), and the
National Basketball Association (NBA) was also white.

In 1945, while football in the "White" Texas high schools and colleges
was flourishing in front of capacity crowds and making headlines in
big city newspapers, football was also being played at the hundreds of
Black high schools and in several Black colleges in the state. However,
the football being played at the state's Black schools was far from the
large crowds and big city media. The underfunded Black schools often
couldn't afford proper equipment, training facilities, or playing fields. In
many cases, the Black high schools in a community were handed down
the used uniforms and equipment when the White high school got new
ones. In addition, the Black high schools typically played their games on
Wednesday or Thursday nights when the stadiums owned by the White
high schools were available for rent.[15] The bright Friday night lights were
reserved for the White schools.

When examining the sports pages in Texas newspapers from the
1940s and 1950s, one is struck by the extensive coverage given to both
college and high school football. Large headlines announced upcoming
games and described games just completed. However, rarely is football
in Black schools even mentioned. When it is, the report is likely to be
similar to one found in the *Houston Post* in November 1945. The report
stated that two "well-mannered Negro teams" were going to play, and
that a special section would be reserved for White fans.[16]

However, 1945 was a watershed year for race relations in Texas and the rest of the United States. That year, millions of American soldiers returned home from World War II. During the war, more than one million Black soldiers had served in the US armed forces. A large number of these Black soldiers, having left the ubiquitous segregation of the Jim Crow South for the first time, experienced being treated as equals in foreign countries and were reluctant to return to subservient positions in their home country. World War II was not only a war against a brutal enemy, but also pitted the supposed American ideals of "liberty and justice for all" and "all men are created equal" against Hitler's "master race theory" that categorized Jews, Blacks, and others as "sub-human."[17] While fighting Hitler, many Americans were forced to take a hard look at racial conditions and attitudes in their own country.

The history of segregation in sports is apparent from a brief examination of baseball. During Reconstruction, there are numerous examples of Black and White athletes participating as teammates or opponents in athletic contests. In 1872, then fourteen-year-old Bud Fowler became the first Black professional baseball player by joining a barnstorming team in New Castle, Pennsylvania. Several other Black professional baseball players followed.[18] The end of Reconstruction meant the end of opportunities for Black athletes as well. Bud Fowler and other Black athletes were soon forced off White teams. In 1895, Fowler stated in *Sporting Life*, a weekly newspaper, "My skin is against me. If I had not been quite so Black, I might have caught on as a Spaniard or something of that kind. The race prejudice is so strong that my Black skin barred me."[19]

By the early decades of the twentieth century, baseball reigned as the unchallenged national pastime. As part of a "gentleman's agreement," Blacks were totally excluded from participating in Major League Baseball or any of its recognized minor leagues during the first half of the century. Thus, while White stars like Babe Ruth, Ty Cobb, and Lou Gehrig basked in the national limelight, Black athletes were barred from participation. Black athletes with the talent and interest to attempt to make a living at baseball were forced to play in the Negro leagues or on barnstorming teams.[20]

Despite these limitations, Black baseball developed stars of indisputable talent who could have excelled in any league at any time. Some of the more prominent stars included pitcher Satchel Paige, catcher Josh

Gibson, infielder Ray Dandridge, and outfielder James "Cool Papa" Bell. Perhaps the words of Black sportswriter Sam Lacy, written in 1945, best summarize the era of segregated baseball. He said, "Baseball has given employment to known epileptics, kleptomaniacs, and a generous scattering of saints and sinners. A man who is totally lacking in character has turned out to be a star in baseball. A man whose skin is white or red or yellow has been acceptable. But a man whose character may be of the highest and whose ability may be Ruthian has been barred completely from the sport because he is colored."[21]

The transition began on October 24, 1945. At a press conference in Montreal, the Brooklyn Dodgers announced that they had signed Jackie Robinson to a baseball contract and assigned him to the Montreal Royals, their top minor league team. It is said that this news hit those in attendance like a thunderbolt.[22] For the first time in the history of modern baseball, a Black man was going to compete in a formerly all-White game.

Opponents of baseball integration made three primary arguments.[23] The first was that there were simply no Black players with the ability to play in the major leagues. In a letter to New York Mayor Fiorello LaGuardia in 1945, Yankee president Larry MacPhail stated, "There are few, if any, negro players who could qualify for play in the major leagues at this time. A major league player must have something besides natural ability. . . . In conclusion: I have no hesitancy in saying that the Yankees have no intention of signing negro players under contract or reservation to negro clubs."[24]

A second argument against integration was that Blacks had their own leagues, and if the best players from these leagues were taken it would almost certainly mean the end of Negro League baseball. Finally, it was argued that the presence of Black players would offend White fans and hurt attendance.

The man with the courage and foresight to test these assumptions and overturn segregated baseball was Branch Rickey, general manager of the Brooklyn Dodgers. Rickey's decision to sign the unproven Negro League rookie Jackie Robinson as the person to break the race barrier ahead of the more established stars in the Negro leagues was not haphazard. Jackie Robinson had served as a second lieutenant in the army and was an excellent all-around athlete. He had attended integrated public schools in his hometown of Pasadena, California, before lettering in football, baseball, basketball, and track at UCLA. After the war, he earned a place on the powerhouse Kansas City Monarchs of the Negro League where he was identified by Rickey and signed to a minor league contract in 1945. Rickey considered Robinson to be educated, articulate, disciplined, and accustomed to interracial competition, making him the perfect public figure for Rickey's project of integration. Robinson was a devoted husband and, in common with Rickey, a devout Presbyterian, which Rickey trusted would make Robinson more immune from the vices that, in the caricatured public imagination of the era, stalked other Negro League stars.

Robinson proved to be the ideal person for the job. After a year in the minor leagues with Montreal, Robinson joined the Brooklyn Dodgers in 1947. In his first year with the Dodgers, Robinson was named National League Rookie of Year and led the Dodgers to the World Series. His ensuing ten-year career earned him a place in baseball's Hall of Fame. Robinson's heroics opened the door, and within a few years many other Black players, such as Willie Mays and Henry Aaron, were in MLB.

The racial climate in other professional sports was not greatly different from that of baseball. There were a few Black professional football players early in the twentieth century, but there were none in the NFL between 1934 and 1945. In 1946, four Black players entered the NFL—Kenny Washington and Woody Strode of the Los Angeles Rams and Marion Motley and Bill Willis of the Cleveland Browns. When the National Basketball Association was established in the early 1940s, all players were White. The NBA broke the race barrier in 1950 when Nat "Sweetwater" Clifton played for the New York Knicks, Chuck Cooper played for the Boston Celtics, and Earl Lloyd played for the Washington Capitols.

In contrast to professional sports, the partial integration of college sports took place early, following regional patterns. In college football, for example, many colleges in the North, Midwest, and West were already racially integrated and began to integrate their football teams nearly as early as they began to play football. Other schools in these regions resisted integration and had no Black players for decades. Black athletes were generally few, and their treatment was often harsh, but they nevertheless did participate. George Jewett became the first Black football player at the University of Michigan in 1890 and soon became an established star. Other early outstanding Black college football players included Frederick Douglass "Fritz" Pollard of Brown, and Fred "Duke" Slater and Oze Simmons (from Texas) of the University of Iowa. Paul Robeson was an all-American at Rutgers in 1917 and 1918. Robeson's career was evidence of the unfair treatment Black athletes faced in that era. In 1916, Rutgers was scheduled to play Washington and Lee College from Virginia. When Washington and Lee objected to playing against Robeson, the Rutgers president ordered that he be benched. Jack Trice integrated the Iowa State football team in 1923. In one game against Minnesota, he suffered a broken collarbone but kept playing. Later, he was hit hard by three Minnesota players and had to be carried off the field on a stretcher. Two days later he died of internal bleeding and a ruptured lung. In 1975, the new football stadium at Iowa State University was named in his honor. In the early 1940s, UCLA had an excellent football team led by three Black players—Kenny Washington, Woody Strode, and Jackie Robinson. As mentioned earlier, Washington and Strode helped reintegrate the NFL by signing with the Los Angeles Rams in 1946.[25] While he was an all-American football player, Jackie Robinson's destiny was in baseball.

In contrast to the integration occurring in other parts of the country, the South remained a Jim Crow dream. The integration of professional sports was made possible by the fact that there were no major league professional teams in the Deep South at that time, when formalized legal segregation was the law. After baseball integrated, major league teams were careful to assign their Black minor league players to leagues in the North. However, the realm of Jim Crow was weakening, and sports were becoming an important agent for change. In 1949, as the integrated Brooklyn Dodgers broke their spring training camp in Florida, they scheduled exhibition games in several cities as they moved north. Some of these cities had never had interracial competition, and several had laws forbidding such games. The economic success of these games was astonishing, and attendance records were set at each stop. This included overflow crowds in both Dallas and Fort Worth.[26]

In 1952, the Dallas Eagles, a minor league baseball team in the Texas League, signed their first Black player, becoming the first integrated sports team in Texas. By 1955, the Texas League was fully integrated. Also in 1952, the New York Yankees, a struggling NFL franchise, moved to Dallas and became the Dallas Texans. The Texans were the state's first fully integrated major professional league franchise. The franchise only lasted one year, and pro football didn't return to Texas until 1960.

While the façade was cracking, the schools of the Southwest Conference and other conferences in the South prohibited Black students and thus Black athletes. Integration of college sports would represent not merely ending segregation on a particular team or league, but in the entire public education system. To many university administrators, the idea of Black players on the football teams was unthinkable since the football team was the most visible symbol of the university. The emergence of integration as a national issue provoked a backlash in the South that resulted in southern schools refusing to schedule intersectional games with opponents that had even a single Black player. At other times, games would be scheduled and played only if the opponent agreed to have their Black players sit out.

Prior to integration, intersectional football games between southern and northern teams were packed with special meaning for southerners. In a way, people in the South saw these games as a rematch of the Civil War. The games represented an arena to show the rest of the country the fallacy of the image they held of the South as backward and populated by mental and physical defectives.[27] Following the 1925 season, the University of Alabama was invited to play in the Rose Bowl on January 1, 1926, against heavily favored Washington. Alabama's 20–19 win was celebrated throughout the South. In the 1929 Rose Bowl, Georgia Tech defeated California 8–7, cementing the strength of southern football. Despite the great benefits of the intersectional games, preserving racial boundaries was even more important, and games wouldn't be played unless northern squads agreed to not play their Black players.

There were exceptions and breakthroughs, again demonstrating that sports could be an agent for change. In the late 1930s, North Carolina, Maryland, and Duke all played games against a northern school with Black players. SMU, TCU, and Texas A&M all traveled to California to play against an integrated UCLA team. During this era, integrated teams were never invited to play in the South. In 1955, the Georgia Tech University football team had accepted an invitation to play against the University of Pittsburgh in the Sugar Bowl in New Orleans. After accepting the invitation, Georgia Tech officials learned that Pittsburgh had a lone Black player, a reserve running back named Bobby Grier, on their team. Upon hearing this news, Georgia's governor issued a statement that Georgia Tech would not play in the game. The governor was further infuriated because Sugar Bowl officials had agreed to allow Pittsburgh fans to be seated on a nonsegregated basis. In response to the governor's statement, a "howling mob of Georgia Tech students formed, broke through police lines, and broke windows in the governor's office." A shaken governor learned that segregation may be fine in his opinion, but don't let it get in the way of football.[28] The game was played and became the first integrated bowl game in the Deep South. Similarly, in 1963, the Mississippi State basketball team earned an invitation to play in the NCAA Tournament. Their first opponent would be Loyola of Chicago, which had several Black players. The Mississippi legislature consequently forbade the team from playing. Because of opposition to playing against an opponent with a Black player, Mississippi State had previously declined invitations to play in the NCAA Tournament in 1959, 1961, and 1962. Coach Babe McCarthy, however, had had enough. This time he snuck his team out of town and played the game anyway.

In the Southwest Conference, this policy of refusing to play teams with Black players in Texas was abandoned in 1948 when Penn State brought two Black players to compete against SMU in the Cotton Bowl. This was the first integrated major college football game in the state of Texas. The Nittany Lions, however, were forced to stay at the Naval Air Station to avoid dealing with segregated Dallas accommodations.[29]

Chapter Two

The Beginnings of School Integration

Before the integration of school sports could occur, school segregation policies had to be overcome. The Supreme Court decision in *Brown v. Board of Education* of 1954 was an important landmark in a long journey of incremental legal gains. In fact, the legality of segregated schools had been gradually eroding for about two decades.[1] Starting in the 1930s, the National Association for the Advancement of Colored People (NAACP) began filing lawsuits challenging the separate-but-equal doctrine. In these cases, evidence was presented showing that in practice separate-but-equal always meant inferior Black schools and discrimination against Black people. The first important case, *Murray v. Pearson*, occurred in 1935 when a Black student named Donald Murray sought admission to the University of Maryland Law School. At this time there were no law schools in the state for Blacks. Maryland, which was one of four slave states that remained in the Union during the Civil War, enacted extensive Jim Crow laws after Reconstruction, including segregated schools. Like other southern states, Maryland had granted out-of-state scholarships to Black students for programs that were not available in the state's segregated Black schools. Lawyers in the Murray case included Charles Hamilton Houston and future Supreme Court Justice Thurgood Marshall. The Maryland Court of Appeals ruled that the state must provide equal opportunity within its own institutions. Rather than go to the expense of developing a law school in the state's Black college, the University of Maryland Law School admitted Murray.

In 1937 and 1938, President Franklin Delano Roosevelt appointed Hugo Black of Alabama and Stanley Reed of Kentucky, two White southerners who favored desegregation, to the Supreme Court. With a newly installed liberal majority, the pace of judicial rulings in favor of desegregation began to accelerate. In 1938, the court followed the same principle as *Murray* when Lloyd Gaines, a Black person from Missouri, sought admission to the University of Missouri Law School. In *Gaines v. Canada*, the court ruled that the state had to furnish within its borders educational facilities for Blacks that were substantially equal to facilities available to Whites. A sidelight to this story is that a year later, Gaines went missing, and his fate remains a mystery.

The Supreme Court went further in 1948 in ruling that not only must equal facilities be available for both races, but they must be made available to one applicant as soon as for another. This 1948 case involved Ada Lois Sipuel, a Black woman who sought admission to the University of Oklahoma Law School. When the state considered developing a law school for Blacks, the court ruled in *Sipuel v. Board of Regents of the University of Oklahoma* that this was not soon enough and ordered that she be admitted to the University of Oklahoma. While Sipuel was admitted, she was treated much differently than the other students. Differential treatment at the University of Oklahoma also occurred when George McLaurin was admitted to the university as a graduate student. A cubicle was built in the classrooms and cafeteria so that McLaurin would be out of sight of the other students. He was also provided with a separate restroom and given a desk to study in the library that was out of sight of the other students. Then in 1950, the Supreme Court in *McLaurin v. Oklahoma State Regents* ruled that the university could not be internally segregated, and that students of one race must be given the same treatment as students of another race.

Another important case involved the State of Texas. In 1946, Herman Sweatt, a Black man from Yates High School in Houston, applied for admission to the University of Texas Law School. He was denied, and in the ensuing court case, the Texas Supreme Court gave the state six months to develop a law school for Black students at Texas Southern, a segregated Black school in Houston. Sweatt, however, claimed the schools were not equal and refused to enroll at Texas Southern. Eventually his case reached the Supreme Court. In *Sweatt v. Painter*, the court ruled unanimously in favor of Sweatt and ordered that he be admitted to the University of Texas. The court stated:

The University of Texas Law School possesses to a far greater degree those qualities which are incapable of objective measurement but which make for greatness in a law school. Such qualities, to name but a few, include reputation of the faculty, experience of the administration, position and influence of the alumni, standing in the community, tradition and prestige.

Thus, through the years the legal status of segregation was gradually eroding. Finally, in 1952 the Supreme Court agreed to consider five cases that directly challenged the separate-but-equal policy and questioned whether segregation itself was a condition of inequality. All five cases involved elementary and secondary schools. For two years the Supreme Court carefully considered the issues. On May 17, 1954, the court issued what is perhaps the most important decree in the battle for racial integration in US history. In a unanimous opinion, the court stated in *Brown v. Board of Education*, "We conclude that in the field of public education the doctrine of 'separate but equal' has no place. Separate facilities are inherently unequal."

Reactions to the court's decision varied widely throughout the South. In some border states—where segregation was not as firmly entrenched in the social order, the Black population was relatively small, and the economic advantages of operating one rather than two schools were apparent—desegregation began soon after the court decision and the process moved quickly. At the other extreme, the states in the Deep South strongly protested the Brown decision, and in six states (Alabama, Georgia, Louisiana, Mississippi, North Carolina, and South Carolina) statutes were instigated that would require the abolition of the public school system if integration was to proceed.

Because of the tremendous size and diversity of the state of Texas, responses to the *Brown* decision varied greatly. The major media outlets advocated a calm approach, and many politicians stated that they thought integration could take place if given time. The May 18, 1954, edition of the *Houston Post* included the reaction of several Houston residents. The majority supported integration and felt it could work. A few, however, felt otherwise. For example, Martha Ann Pool, age 19, stated, "I'm definitely against it. I think it's terrible." J. W. F. Lieck, a retiree, said, "If Dwight D. Eisenhower and the Supreme Court judges don't think they're any better than Negroes, they ought to resign their jobs and give them to Negroes." Mrs. W. T. Magee Cage, age 39, added, "It will never, never work. I don't think it will happen in Texas."

The First Decade of School Desegregation in Texas

Not surprisingly, reactions in Texas to the Supreme Court's *Brown* decision were most favorably received in South Texas and West Texas, and most negatively received in East Texas. In the southern and western parts of the state, the Black population was less than 2 percent of the total in many counties, and decision-makers were well aware of the extensive costs of providing separate schools for a handful of Black students. Further, many school districts in those areas had large Hispanic populations. The question of segregating Hispanics in public schools had been fought in Texas courts, with the result being that Whites and Hispanics, by law, could attend the same schools. There were cases, however, where separate schools were constructed for Hispanic students during this time period. But by Texas law at the time, if you were not Black then you were considered White. Thus, in the view of many, the schools were already integrated and adding a few Black kids where there were already large numbers of Hispanic kids was not considered a major issue. Texas law defined race as binary—you were either Black or White—when it is, in fact, far more complex.

Although it was not widely known at the time, Friona, a rural school district in the Texas Panhandle had enrolled a small handful of Black students in schools with White students in 1954. This occurred because a migrant farm worker named Robert Walker, his wife, and their three elementary aged children moved into the community. There were no other Black students in the town and building a school and hiring a teacher for these three kids were economically prohibitive. To address the problem, school Superintendent Robert Caffey quietly enrolled the three students in Friona Elementary.[2] Thus, it was in Friona in 1954 that Black and White students attended the same public school in Texas for the first time in the twentieth century.[3]

Soon after the Supreme Court decision, many schools in South Texas and West Texas began making plans to desegregate. Prior to the 1954–55 school year, a few Black students applied for admission to White schools throughout the state. All were denied. At the time, the Gilmer-Aikens Act of 1949 required the separation of races in public schools. Gilmer-Aikens was the most recent in a series of Texas laws requiring segregated schools, and failure to comply with the law could result in the loss of state funds. While school districts awaited word from the state, the state reported that it was waiting for the Supreme Court to specify desegregation procedures.

Meanwhile, the platform adopted at the 1954 Texas Democratic Convention declared that the Supreme Court decision was an "unwarranted invasion" of state's rights. In the fall of 1954, Texas Governor Allen Shivers won reelection on a platform that included continued segregation. He maintained that the operation of public schools was best managed by the state, and the Supreme Court decision represented an unwarranted federal intrusion into what was the jurisdiction of the state. Also in 1954, the State of Texas sent a brief to the Supreme Court in which they claimed discrimination was the evil to be avoided, not segregation, and that discrimination could best be avoided with separate schools. The state further claimed that Texas had no discrimination, only segregation. A Texas poll at this time showed that 71 percent of respondents were opposed to school integration. Thus, the year following the Brown decision was a period of waiting and watching throughout the state.

On May 31, 1955, the Supreme Court told the states to act "with all deliberate speed" to end segregation. Given no specific timetable, some communities began the endless process of foot dragging. For Texas school districts wishing to integrate, the doors were opened in 1955 when the Texas Supreme Court declared that school districts could continue to draw state funds for desegregated schools. Consequently, in the fall of 1955, about sixty Texas school districts (out of about 1,900 school districts at the time) announced that they were desegregated and that Black students would be admitted to formerly all-White schools. All sixty districts were in South Texas and West Texas. For many of these districts, the costs of operating separate schools for a small number of Black students were prohibitive, and many of these districts jumped at the opportunity to integrate. In the West Texas town of San Saba, for example, the few Black students were required to make an eighty-five-mile round trip bus ride to Brady each day to attend Brady's segregated

Black school because San Saba couldn't afford to operate separate schools of their own for their few Black students. Thus, San Saba schools were fully integrated in the fall of 1955.

One of the districts that moved to integrate was San Antonio Independent School District, where Black students comprised less than 8 percent of the total and were greatly outnumbered by both White and Hispanic students. The September 1, 1955, edition of the *San Antonio Express* reported, "Integration went off smoothly in the Bexar County schools Wednesday as negro students answered the same bell as white pupils for the first time." The transition to integrated schools in San Antonio was gradual and incomplete. For example, in 1955 integration in San Antonio schools was allowed in only the first, second, seventh, and tenth grades. Students who had attended one year at a particular school, whether Black or White, had to return to that same school. However, students of either race who had just finished junior high could choose to attend any of the eight high schools in the district. The same was true for those entering elementary or junior high for the first time, as they could choose to attend any school in the district. In actuality, there were very few Black students who attended classes with White students in 1955 in San Antonio or elsewhere in Texas. Most Black students in San Antonio continued to attend the legally desegregated but still almost exclusively Black schools located in the East and Northeast neighborhoods where most of them lived.

In some rural districts in parts of the state with few Black students, the dual Black and White schools were abandoned, and all of the Black students were admitted to the White school. After the initial surge in 1955, the number of schools embracing an integration policy and the number of Black students who attended integrated schools increased only gradually in the state, and all the integration that occurred was in southern and western Texas. In virtually every case where Black students started attending White schools, they became aware of the vast differences in facilities and available programs and realized that separate but equal was a sham. It was apparent that everything in the White school, from the classrooms to the textbooks, was better than what had been available to them in their segregated Black schools. There are cases where unequal treatment continued after desegregation. In some cases, the Black kids were forced to sit at the back of the classroom, some schools put Black and White students in different classrooms even though they were in the same school, and some schools continued to have separate proms and other activities for the Black and White students.[4]

In East Texas, integration patterns were very different. In this part of the state—where the Black population comprised over 40 percent of residents in some counties—segregation was more deeply entrenched, and orders for integration posed a much greater threat to the established social order. For example, in July of 1954, Hardy Ridge, the head of the NAACP in Sulphur Springs, Texas, petitioned the school board to admit Black students to the community's previously all-White schools. About a week later, two shotgun blasts and seven pistol shots were fired into the Ridge home, which fortunately was empty at the time. Other Black people in the neighborhood were told that this was what happens to "uppity niggers," and that people in town didn't like people in Washington telling them what to do. Fearing for their lives, Ridge and his wife moved to Cleveland, Ohio.[5] A decade later, Sulphur Springs schools remained segregated.

In the East Texas community of Tatum, the White students attended Tatum School, while the Black students attended Mayflower School. Like most southern communities, the Black residents of Tatum were forced to live in completely separate neighborhoods. Often the Black community was literally on the other side of the railroad tracks. While the number of students in each school was nearly equal, the quality of the two schools was not. Facilities, books, and classrooms at Mayflower School were all clearly inferior to those at Tatum School. Mayflower School even had far fewer teachers per student than Tatum School.

Following the *Brown* decision, the all-White Tatum school board voted to set aside funds to improve Mayflower School. The intent was to improve the school to the point that it would reduce the likelihood that residents of the Black community would wish to enroll at Tatum school. However, a number of White people were upset that desegregation was even being considered, and they didn't want to spend any more money on Black education. On a Saturday night in the summer of 1955, two young White men, Perry Dean Ross and Joe Reagan Simpson, drove through the Black part of town firing guns at Mayflower School and at the homes and businesses of Black people. John Earl Reese, age 16, was hit in the head and died from one of the shots. Ross and Simpson admitted to firing the shots and were convicted of murder by an all-White jury. Following the conviction, the defense attorney suggested that the jury should just recognize that the boys had a bad day and let them go and live their lives. The all-White jury agreed, and neither Ross nor Simpson ever spent a day in jail for the murder. More than a decade later Tatum schools remained totally segregated.

Another important integration clash occurred in Mansfield, Texas, a community about fifteen miles from Fort Worth. At that time, the City of Mansfield had around 1,450 residents; about 350 of them were Black. Today, Mansfield is a suburb in the Dallas-Fort Worth metro area, but in the 1950s it was more of a separate community. A 1956 editorial in the local newspaper, the *Mansfield News*, clearly expresses the racial attitudes of the era. It stated, "We are not against the Negro, but we are against social equality. We think the Negroes are making great strides in improving their race, and commend them for it, as long as they stick to their race." In Mansfield in the 1950s, Black students from first through eighth grade attended Mansfield Colored School. This school consisted of two long, barrack-like buildings with no electricity, running water, or plumbing. Only one teacher was hired for all eight grades, water was brought in with milk cans, and there were two outhouses. Mansfield's Black students in grades nine through twelve were bused to Fort Worth to attend Terrell High, a segregated Black school in the city. Students caught the commercial Trailways Bus at 7:15 a.m. from Mansfield. This bus took them to the commercial bus center in Fort Worth. From there the students had to walk twenty blocks to the high school. After school, the process was repeated in reverse. However, school ended at 3:30 p.m., and the bus back to Mansfield didn't leave Fort Worth until 5:30.[6]

On July 26, 1955, a petition was submitted to the Mansfield School Board requesting an end to segregated schools. During the next board meeting, the segregation issue was discussed, after which the all-White school board passed a motion to keep the schools segregated. In response, a class action lawsuit was filed in US Federal District Court in Fort Worth on behalf of three Black Mansfield teenagers. Several months later, on August 25, 1956, the court ruled that the minor plaintiffs had the right to attend Mansfield High School on the same basis as the White race. This was the first time a Texas school had been ordered to integrate by the courts.

The response in Mansfield was dramatic. On the night of August 28, an effigy was hung at the main intersection in town. A sign attached to the effigy stated, "This Negro tried to enter a white school." On August 30, another effigy was hung from the flagpole in front of Mansfield High School. The next day, August 31, was when students were expected to come to the school to register for the coming academic year. A crowd of several hundred white residents gathered at Mansfield High to prevent any Black students from registering. One of the protesters declared, "If God had wanted us to go to school together, He wouldn't have made them Black and us white." Among the signs in the crowd were, "We don't want niggers, this is a white school," and, "A dead nigger is the best nigger."[7]

In response to the protests, Texas Governor Shivers ordered the Texas Rangers to Mansfield to preserve the peace. The presence of the Rangers was intended not to provide a safe escort for Black students but to keep Black students out of the school and preserve segregation[8]. Shivers then issued a proclamation that the school should transfer away any student, "white or colored, whose attendance or attempts to attend Mansfield High School would be reasonably calculated to incite violence." In essence, Black students asserting their legal rights were blamed for any potential ensuing violence.[9] Black Mansfield residents then requested help and protection from President Eisenhower. Their pleas, however, were ignored. As a result, Mansfield schools remained segregated, and Black students were still being bused to Fort Worth a decade later. Eisenhower, however, received extensive negative feedback for his lack of action in Mansfield. Consequently, a year later when similar events were occurring at Central High in Little Rock, Arkansas, Eisenhower sent federal troops to assure the safety of the Black students.[10]

In 1957, the Texas legislature passed a law aimed at preserving segregation. This law prohibited desegregation by a school district from occurring without prior approval by a majority of the voters living in the district. The penalty for violation of this law was the loss of state funds. This law proved effective in slowing the integration process. Eventually, federal courts made this law irrelevant.

In sum, during the decade following the 1954 Supreme Court *Brown* decision, the transition from segregated to desegregated schools in Texas moved at a turtle's pace following some initial action in 1955. In 1964, only 3 percent of the Black students in Texas were attending the same school as a single White or even Latino student, with the other 97 percent still attending all-Black schools.[11] This was despite the fact that numerous school districts claimed the policy of integration.

Across the state, three major patterns were followed with respect to school integration: compliance, tokenism, and defiance. Examples of each pattern are apparent in the communities described below.

Brownwood—Compliance

During the 1950s, about 4 percent of the twenty thousand residents of the West Texas community of Brownwood were Black. All K–12 Black students in the city attended Hardin School. In 1954 there were 115 students at Hardin School, twenty-five of whom were in ninth through twelfth grades. After the state made integration possible, the Brownwood Board of Education met on July 25, 1955, and unanimously approved a motion to integrate Brownwood High School. In the fall of 1955, all Black high school students in the city began attending Brownwood High. Hardin remained operating as an elementary school for a few more years before it was closed, and all Brownwood schools were fully integrated. A critical factor in the decision to integrate was the extensive cost of operating a separate school for a relatively small number of Black students.

Odessa—Tokenism

In the 1950s, Odessa was a West Texas city of about thirty thousand residents. The city would soon experience rapid growth due to the development of the oil industry in the Permian Basin, where Odessa is located. Today, Odessa has more than one hundred thousand residents. Like most West Texas communities, Odessa had a relatively small Black population, comprising less than 5 percent of the population. Although most West Texas high schools were relatively quick to integrate, Odessa clung to its segregated school system for as long as possible. When strict segregation was no longer possible, the school district implemented a policy of tokenism based on a freedom of choice plan. The Black high school in Odessa, Blackshear High, did not close until 1966. When Blackshear High did close, nearly all of the Black students in the city began attending Ector High, which at the time was predominately Hispanic. De facto segregation was easily implemented because strict redlining had resulted in all of the Black and Hispanic students living in the same section of the city. Thus, nearly all students at Ector were either Black or Hispanic. In 1981, twenty-seven years after *Brown*, the district closed Ector High, and the Ector students were distributed to the two predominately White high schools in the city, Odessa High and Permian High.

It is also important to note that it was the minority school, Ector, that was closed. This meant that the minority community lost their neighborhood school, and it was minority students who had to be bused across town. Further, many minority teachers and administrators lost their jobs. Permian was the traditional football power, and the new boundaries to distribute Ector students were drawn so that Permian football would benefit from talented student athletes in the city's Black neighborhoods.[12]

Houston—Tokenism

The Houston Independent School District (HISD) was created in 1924.[13] As required by Texas law, district schools were racially segregated. During the 1920s, most Black residents in Houston lived in the highly segregated Third, Fourth, and Fifth Wards, required by the city's redlining policies. When HISD was created, there was only one high school, located in the Fourth Ward, for all of the Black students in the city. The school, which was very overcrowded, was called "Colored High School." In 1926, two additional Black high schools were opened—Yates High in the Third Ward and Wheatley High in the Fifth Ward. Colored High in the Fourth Ward was renamed Booker T. Washington High.

During the middle decades of the twentieth century, the Houston metro area grew rapidly as the city became the international hub of the oil industry and a major petrochemical center. Many Black families from rural Texas moved to Houston to take advantage of better economic opportunities in the booming city. Additional segregated high schools were built to deal with the growing population. By 1955 there were nine Black high schools in the city, and HISD was the largest segregated school system in the country. Following *Brown*, it soon became clear that HISD would strongly resist integration efforts. On February 27, 1956, HISD held a board meeting to discuss school integration. When the topic of integration was first mentioned, a large crowd attending the board meeting started singing "Dixie."

In September 1956, two Black students—fourteen-year-old Beneva Williams and nine-year-old Delores Ross—attempted to enroll at White schools near their homes. Both were turned away. In response, the NAACP filed a lawsuit, *Ross v. HISD*. The District Court for the Southern District of Texas subsequently ruled that the city's segregated school system was unlawful and ordered the district to integrate by 1960. To meet the court's requirement, HISD eventually implemented a freedom of choice plan where students in some neighborhoods could choose to attend either the White school or the Black school nearest their home. The result was that in the fall of 1960, a total of twelve Black elementary students were attending three previously all-White schools. Although this was but a miniscule share of the students in the district, HISD maintained that its schools were desegregated. Throughout the 1960s, HISD continued to claim it had integrated schools, when in reality well over 95 percent of Black students were attending schools where there was not a single White student, and all White students were attending schools where there were few if any Black students.[14] Integrating Houston schools was made more difficult because of the extensive segregation of Houston neighborhoods.

Aldine Independent School District neighbors HISD to the north. The school district was created in 1935. Prior to *Brown*, Aldine High was operated as a White high school, while Carver High was the district's Black high school. In 1964, a full decade after *Brown*, George Franklin Sampson attempted to enroll his children at Aldine High. He was denied and told his children must attend Carver High. Sampson filed suit, and in *Sampson and the United States v. Aldine ISD*, the district court ruled in favor of Sampson and required Aldine schools to integrate. In response, the district also implemented a "freedom of choice" plan where students could choose to attend either Aldine High or Carver High. The consequence was that nearly all students at Aldine High were White and all students at Carver were Black. This situation continued until 1977.

Dallas—Tokenism

Events in Dallas were similar to those in Houston. At the time of the *Brown* decision, Dallas had one of the largest segregated school systems in the nation. Immediately after *Brown*, the district made clear its intentions to remain segregated. This was initially supported by federal judges such as William H. Atwell, chief judge of the US District Court for the Northern District of Texas. Fear of lawsuits, however, prompted the district to adopt a "Stairstep Plan" in 1961. This plan stated that all DISD schools would begin desegregation one grade level per year, beginning with the first grade. As a consequence, in the fall of 1961, eighteen Black students entered previously all-White DISD schools. In 1967, DISD declared its schools were desegregated despite the fact that 159 of the 180 schools in the district were one-race schools where at least 90 percent of the students at the school were either White, Black, or Hispanic.

Beaumont—Defiance

The East Texas city of Beaumont, located near the Louisiana border, has deep roots in the Old South, with near equal numbers of Black and White residents. The region grew rapidly after the discovery of oil at Spindletop in 1901 and remains an important oil producing and oil refining area with a substantial petrochemical industry. Traditionally, the schools and even residential areas were strictly segregated. The west side of town was virtually all White. The nearby towns of Vidor and Nederland were known as "Sundown" towns where no Black people were allowed after sunset. Decades later, in 1993, attempts to integrate public housing in Vidor were met by Ku Klux Klan marches. Indicative of race relations in the Beaumont area was a race riot that occurred on June 15, 1943. At that time, there were false rumors that a Black man had raped a White woman. In response, over two thousand White laborers stormed out of the Beaumont shipyards and assaulted the Black section of town. By morning, three Black people were dead, hundreds injured, and two hundred homes and businesses destroyed. With news of the *Brown* court decision in 1954, Beaumont, like other East Texas communities, was defiant and maintained that its schools would remain segregated. Consequently, for years after the *Brown* decision, Beaumont schools were strictly segregated.

Desegregation in Other Southern States

Although some violence did occur in Texas in the first decade of desegregation, the process was smoother than in some other southern states. The integration of Central High School in Little Rock, Arkansas, in 1957 mentioned earlier involved nine Black students who were attempting to enroll in a previously segregated White school, Central High School. Arkansas Governor Orval Faubus sent the Arkansas National Guard to prevent the Black students from entering the school. President Eisenhower then sent federal troops to escort the students into the school. In other parts of the South, schools that had been ordered to admit Black students were closed. Medgar Evans, an NAACP representative, was shot to death in Jackson, Mississippi, in 1963 after a desegregation strategy meeting. In September 1963, several people were killed and numerous other people injured in Birmingham, Alabama, during riots that ensued as a result of efforts to desegregate schools there. In Macon County, Alabama, when thirteen Black students were admitted to a previously all-White high school, all the White students withdrew. One Black student was subsequently expelled for disciplinary reasons, leaving the school with twelve students and thirteen faculty members. The school operated this way for several months before it was eventually closed for economic reasons.[15]

These painful and often slow-moving events had resulted in the integration of some schools, and the stage was set for integration to occur in Texas high school football. It is to these events that we now turn.

Chapter Three

Texas High School Football
Prior to Integration

Some Texas high school football stories are legendary. In communities all over the state, the games take on epic meaning, and the sixteen- and seventeen-year-old boys in those Friday night battles gain near mythical stature in their communities. In Texas, high school football often actually defines how a town feels about itself. In his classic book, *Friday Night Lights*, Buzz Bissinger was writing about Odessa, but his statement could apply to many Texas communities: "Football stood at the very core of what the town was about. It had nothing to do with entertainment and everything about how people feel about themselves."[1] The exploits of Friday night football heroes are told and retold around the state, and many have gone on to gain national fame.[2] Texas schoolboy players such as Sammy Baugh of Sweetwater, Earl Campbell of John Tyler High in Tyler, Eric Dickerson of Sealy, Billy Sims of Hooks, Johnny Manziel of Kerrville Tivy High, Patrick Mahomes of Whitehouse, and Kyler Murray of Allen need no introduction anywhere in the football world.

The first high school football game in the state was played in 1894. Galveston Ball High School assembled a team that was not school sponsored and consisted of both teachers and students from the school. They lost their first game 14–6 to the Agricultural and Mechanical College of Texas, now Texas A&M University.[3] The first game between two high school teams occurred in Dallas in 1900. The teams were not school supported, and in fact they were not allowed to participate on school grounds. The players' mothers made their uniforms, which were stuffed with cotton to serve as padding.[4]

From these humble beginnings, the sport grew rapidly. In 2018, 1,514 Texas public high schools and 169,288 Texas kids were playing high school football in places ranging from Houston to Hermleigh, from San Antonio to Smyer, and from Dallas to Dalhart. Some high school football stadiums in the state compare favorably to college stadiums in other parts of the country. Ratcliff Stadium in Odessa seats over nineteen thousand. Eagle Stadium in Allen cost $60 million to build and seats eighteen thousand. Katy Independent School District has a football stadium that cost over $70 million to build. Schools without enough students to field a regular eleven-man team play in a six-man league. Virtually every small- to medium-sized town in the state features a welcome sign at the city limits that lists the championships and playoff appearances of the local high school, a prominent water tower painted with the school colors and logo, and a Dairy Queen where the latest football team photo is displayed at the entrance. An old saying in the state is that you know people are serious about religion in Texas because it is sometimes compared in importance with high school football.

Many colorful stories exist about Texas high school football in the early days. In 1905, the Texas Interscholastic Athletic Association was organized to attempt to bring order to the chaos that high school sports were becoming. The association had only four eligibility rules, and few people paid much attention to them. The contestant had to be amateur, twenty-one years old or less, have a three-month attendance record in the school he represented, and be passing three courses. Some young men made a career out of high school football, playing five or six years. One Ranger High player was reported to have been married with two children. Once, a high school player in Fort Worth was declared ineligible because it was found that he had two years of college football experience. Sudden transfers by students and recruiting by coaches were common. By the 1920s, the only residence rule was that a player's parents must reside in the school district as of September 1. Naturally, ambitious coaches, supported by the promise of jobs from local businesses, began recruiting players and moving families. Sportswriter Boyce House elected the Cisco High team as his all-state team in the 1920s. Cisco was a booming oil town west of Fort Worth where oil money was flowing freely at the time. Listing each member of the team and the town he had originally come from, House concluded that only one player was actually from Cisco, and that the team fairly well represented the state.[5]

Obviously, Texas high school coaches and supporters were willing to go to great lengths to assure that they put the best possible football team on the field. However, for decades a vast pool of potentially great football players was totally excluded—the Black Texans. Further, while millions of young boys growing up in Texas had dreams of leading the local high school football team to glory, young Black boys were relegated to play in relative anonymity on segregated teams. On the White side of the community, kids played organized little league baseball and football on carefully manicured fields with snappy uniforms. Youth sports organizations, swimming pools, and parks were strictly segregated, and few of these opportunities were available on the other side of the tracks where the Black families lived.

In 1910, the University of Texas Interscholastic League—now typically referred to as the University Interscholastic League, or UIL—was formed. In 1920, the UIL took over the operation of high school football in Texas from the Texas Interscholastic Athletic Association. However, as part of the state's "separate but equal" policy, which stated that "separate schools shall be provided for white and colored children," the UIL only recognized the White schools in the state. The hundreds of Black high schools in the state were totally ignored by the UIL and obligated to organize a separate organization. The accomplishments of the exceptional Black athletes and teams that competed in these segregated leagues of the pre-integration era were disregarded at the time and are largely forgotten today.

In 1920, the Black schools of the state organized the "Texas Interscholastic League of Colored Schools" as a corollary of the UIL. The purpose of this organization was to provide an arena for their students to develop skills and abilities. The league sponsored events in all the major sports as well as arithmetic, science, spelling, one-act plays, music, and other subjects. At its peak, the organization served over five hundred schools ranging in size from one-teacher schools to large city schools.[6]

In 1963, the name of the organization was officially changed to "The Prairie View Interscholastic League of Texas," because the offices were housed at the Prairie View A&M College of Texas, now Prairie View A&M University, the state's Black land grant college. Since its founding, it has generally been referred to as the Prairie View League or PVIL. The PVIL faced numerous severe obstacles in providing a quality program for Black secondary students in the state. Most obvious was that the schools that comprised the Prairie View League were severely underfunded, and many of the students were destitute. Despite these obstacles, the Prairie View League ran a quality program for decades.[7] Unfortunately, the records of many of the accomplishments of outstanding young Black athletes and teams of the pre-integration era were destroyed by a fire at Prairie View A&M University in March 1947. The league also never recorded some statistics because of a lack of resources.

Those who remember the early days of Prairie View League football recount a colorful history. Until about midcentury, the league made no attempt to determine district or state champions, and in many parts of the state there were virtually no eligibility rules. The people in one community would round up some players to have a game against the neighboring community. Some athletes continued to play on the high school team years after leaving school. The officials were often unqualified, and controversial calls sometimes lead to near riots. Sportswriter Jimmy Blair told the story about when a home team was trailing 18–14 and had the ball at the visitors ten-yard line with time running out. On the last play of the game, the official called a fifteen-yard piling-on penalty on the visitors and then proceeded to step the penalty off into the end zone for the winning touchdown.[8] By about 1940, the organizational control had improved, and the former coaches and participants remember that a rough, hard-nosed brand of football was played in the Prairie View League. Many great athletes spent their high school days participating in the PVIL. Before he became "Mr. Cub," Ernie Banks played PVIL football for Booker T. Washington High School in Dallas.

During the 1940s and 1950s, Oland Rogers was the coach at Douglass High, the Black school in the East Texas community of Pittsburg. He recalls some hard-nosed football. He also recalls other events that illustrate some of the peculiarities of race relations at the time.[9] One year his team made it to the playoffs and traveled to San Angelo in West Texas to play the Black school there. When his team took the field, they found that the game was being officiated by White officials. This practice was common in West Texas, but unheard of in East Texas. The Douglass High players had extremely limited contact with Whites and were totally intimidated. On another occasion, Douglass High was playing the Black school in Sulphur Springs. Coach Rogers recalls that his team was totally dominating the game but couldn't seem to score a touchdown. He finally found out the reason why. Some White boys were sitting near a clump of bushes near the end zone. They had told the Douglass High players that they had a shotgun hidden in the bushes and they would "shoot the first nigger that scored a touchdown." The situation was remedied by running the White boys off, and Douglass went on to an easy win.

High school football in the White schools typically enjoyed extensive media coverage, state-of-the-art facilities and equipment, and well-paid coaches. High school football in the Black schools had none of these advantages. Further, given the socioeconomic structure of the state at that time, very few Black kids remained in school long enough to play high school football. With most Black families being destitute, the incomes of the children were needed as soon as they were old enough to get a job. In addition, there was little motivation for a young Black person to stay in school since a combination of Jim Crow laws, custom, and discrimination meant the best job most a Black person could hope for was a laborer. About the only opportunities for educated Black people were teaching in the underfunded Black schools and in the ministry.

There are a few rare situations where racial conventions were disrupted in the early days of Texas high school football. In 1923, high school football was started in the tiny West Texas community of Rotan. From the very beginning, the number one fan of Rotan Yellowhammer football was Henry Govan. For sixty-five years, "Mr. H.," as he was known, roamed the sideline for every Rotan High football game, whether at home or on the road. "Mr. H." served as a volunteer trainer and would carry water to the team, handle team equipment, mend minor injuries, tape ankles, and hold the players' watches and wallets during the game. Mr. H. was widely recognized as the conscience of not only the football team, but the entire community as well. What was unusual was that in what was a totally White-man's game, Mr. H. was Black. For the first forty-one years he was associated with Yellowhammer football, Mr. H. had to send his own children out of town to school because Rotan schools were segregated, and the community had no school for Blacks. In an era of a strict racial caste system, Mr. H. tested and broke several racial barriers. He became the first Black landowner in Rotan. He would travel with the team to neighboring communities such as Roby and Throckmorton even though those towns had ordinances prohibiting Black people from being in town after sundown. In the late 1940s, a café owner in Roby told the Rotan team that he would not serve Govan. Upon hearing this, the entire team walked out and left the proprietor with several dozen steaming steaks. In the early 1980s, the football field at Rotan High was named in his honor—the H. Govan Field. On December 15, 1988, Mr. H. died at the age of ninety-one.[10]

Chapter Four

The First Decade of Texas High School Football Integration, 1954–1964

During this first decade of school integration in Texas, Black players and teams won some important battles in the classroom and on the football field in the long and slow struggle for integration and social equality. During the initial decade following *Brown v. Board of Education*, the vast majority of Black students in the state were still attending all-Black schools. Only 3 percent of the Black students in Texas were attending a school with even one White student in 1964. To the credit of the UIL, as soon as integration began in 1955, the organization announced that integrated schools were welcome and that Black students could participate in UIL events as long as their school was sanctioned. In reality, change on the ground was slow throughout the decade, and the huge majority of those participating in UIL sanctioned activities were White, while the vast majority of Black student athletes were still participating in the all-Black Prairie View League.

As some school districts in Texas began to desegregate in 1955, conflicts in high school football were immediate. The September 2, 1955, issue of the *Dallas Morning News* stated, "Texas schoolboy football opens Friday marred by forfeits and desegregation disputes." Because early desegregation efforts were limited to South Texas and West Texas, early disputes were also centered in these parts of the state.

Robstown/Yoakum

One such dispute involved two South Texas high schools, Robstown and Yoakum. Robstown is a community of about ten thousand people located about twenty miles inland from Corpus Christi. As is typical of many

South Texas communities, Robstown has a large Hispanic population, while Blacks comprised less than two percent of the total. During the 1940s, the community had battled over the issue of integration of White and Hispanic students in the same school. One elementary school was all White until the first Hispanic children were admitted in 1949. In the early 1950s, there was an elementary school for Black children in Robstown, but Black high school students were bused to Solomon Coles, the Black high school in Corpus Christi. There were simply not enough Black high school students in Robstown to economically justify the operation of a separate segregated school for them.

According to locals, relations between Black and White people had always been fairly smooth in Robstown. In 1949, W. N. Corder (May 16, 1915–May 29, 1994) was hired as principal at Robstown High.[1] After his arrival, Corder was instrumental in getting Little League baseball organized in the community because he had three sons of Little League age. Corder told me that almost from the outset, Little League baseball in Robstown was integrated with minimal problems. Because of smooth racial relations, and because of the extensive costs of busing high school students to Corpus, Robstown moved quickly to integrate after the *Brown* decision. In the summer of 1955, it was announced that Robstown schools would integrate and that all Black high school students in the community would be admitted to Robstown High.

Coincidentally, among the first Black students admitted to Robstown High were several fine football players and one truly exceptional player, Willie Jones. Community leaders and coaches were aware of Willie Jones prior to the decision to integrate, but when questioned if a desire to have his talents on the football team had anything to do with their desegregation decision, they answered a unanimous no. Everyone interviewed admits, however, that his success certainly helped the integration process go smoother once it had begun. So readily were the Black students accepted at Robstown High that Willie Jones was elected captain of the football team, and another Black student was elected president of the choir during their first year at the school.

Robstown players and coaches were excited about the upcoming football season and were preparing for their season opening game against Yoakum on September 2, 1955. In Yoakum, however, matters on the integration front were not going nearly as smoothly. During the 1950s,

Yoakum was about the same size as Robstown. Yoakum, however, is about one hundred miles north of Robstown and consequently had a substantially larger Black population with a smaller Latino population. In fact, a new Black high school had recently been constructed in the community. Persons who lived in Yoakum during the 1950s described their community racial attitudes with such terms as "extremely prejudiced" and "very bigoted." Community residents tell of an incident that occurred during the 1930s that provides some indication of racial outlooks. At that time, a Black man was accused of raping a White woman. Before the trial, the Black man was removed from the local jail during the night and no trace of him was ever found again. There were never any arrests made in the man's disappearance.

Although some of the communities surrounding Yoakum were integrating their public schools in the fall of 1955, there was strong resistance to do so in Yoakum. In fact, many of the community residents began to be concerned when it became apparent that some of the opponents of their high school football team were going to integrate. What would they do if some of these integrated schools had Black players on their football teams? Concern was especially strong among some players' parents, who were strongly opposed to having their sons participate in an interracial athletic contest. The issue reached a head during the week prior to the Robstown game when they learned there were several Black players on the Robstown team.

In an attempt to deal with the situation and alleviate the confusion, Bobby Goff (June 19, 1926–October 19, 2013) who was the first-year head coach at Yoakum High, called for a vote of his players.[2] The players voted to play the schedule as given. Coach Goff then went to the school board and got approval to play against integrated squads. Despite strong opposition from the parents of some players, it appeared the football season would proceed as scheduled. At this point, school Superintendent George Barron returned from a trip out of town, overruled the school board, and stated that Yoakum would not play against integrated teams. Barron maintained that, if necessary, the school would play a renegade schedule. Barron then called the UIL in an attempt to get out of the contract that Yoakum High had with integrated football schools. His contention was that the opposing schools were segregated when the contracts were made, and that since they had integrated, the contracts were no longer binding.

The UIL had already decided that integrated schools would be accepted as full members of the organization, and thus Yoakum was told they would have to play their contracted schedule.

The town then called a meeting at Yoakum High School to discuss the issue. Not surprisingly, the ensuing meeting was fraught with emotions and tensions. Coach Goff remembers that he and his assistant coaches were called "nigger lovers" because they wanted to play. The decision that emerged from this meeting was that the team would ask its opponents not to play their Black players, and that it would forfeit rather than play against integrated teams. When Robstown refused to leave their Black players out of the game, Yoakum announced that it would forfeit.

In wake of the forfeit to Robstown, the UIL slapped Yoakum High with a $1,900 fine. Given this decision, coupled with the fact that a substantial part of the community wanted to play the games, the school reversed course and decided to play the rest of the football season as scheduled. As each controversy facing the community emerged, the division splitting the town grew wider. Several players, often under pressure from their parents, quit the team when it was apparent that Yoakum would play against integrated teams. Other players, again mostly under parental pressure, said they would play but that they would leave the field if the opponent had a Black player in the game.

After an off week, Yoakum was scheduled to travel to Kenedy High to play against another integrated football team on September 16. Superintendent Barron had contacted the Kenedy school administrators and asked them to keep their Black players out of the game. The rumor around Yoakum that week was Kenedy had agreed to this request. As the game began, it appeared this would indeed be the case, as an all-White Kenedy team took the field. Throughout most of the first quarter, two all-White teams were battling it out. Suddenly, a Black player wearing the Kenedy High uniform trotted from the sideline and entered the Kenedy huddle. Immediately five Yoakum players left the field, refusing to play in a game with the Black participant. Amid the resulting confusion, Coach Goff was forced to call time-out and search for eleven boys willing to play. This pattern continued throughout the game, with a handful of Yoakum players refusing to participate whenever Kenedy had a Black player in the game. Not surprisingly, when the game ended, Kenedy was victorious by a 13–7 score.

The remainder of the 1955 football season in Yoakum would be what Bobby Goff's wife, Billie Jean Goff (March 25, 1929–May 13, 2007), called "a nightmare."[3] The team was weakened by those who quit prior to the Kenedy game and further weakened by the fact that several players would not play when the opponent had a Black player on the field. The turmoil and confusion in the town from the desegregation issue weighed on the team. When the season ended with a loss to Cuero, Yoakum had a record of zero wins and ten losses. In addition to the forfeit to Robstown and the loss to Kenedy, other losses included a 45–6 defeat to Lockhart, a 40–0 thumping from Refugio, and a disastrous 75–0 shellacking by Port Lavaca Calhoun.

Yoakum schools did not integrate until 1964. When Black students first entered Yoakum High, an exceptional football player was included among their numbers—Charlie Hall. Hall was an all-state linebacker at Yoakum, and later became one of the first Black football players at the University of Houston. When the University of Houston entered the Southwest Conference in 1976, the school published its all-time team, and Charlie Hall was featured at linebacker.[4] Hall also played several years in the NFL with the Cleveland Browns.

After the disastrous 1955 season, Bobby Goff coached one more season at Yoakum. He then moved to Goliad and coached there for a couple of seasons before he finally settled in Port Lavaca. At Calhoun High in Port Lavaca, Goff had a very successful coaching career. His 1960 team made it to the state championship game before losing to Brownwood and Coach Gordon Wood. Goff eventually moved into an administrative position in Port Lavaca schools before retiring in 1989. Coach Goff died in 2013, a few years after the passing of his wife of sixty years, Billie Jean. Bobby Goff is also remembered for his playing days at Texas A&M, where he held the school record with an eighty-six-yard punt against Texas Tech.

On September 9, 1955, the week following the Yoakum forfeit, Robstown played against Refugio High and star Black running back James Lott in the first high school football game in Texas history between two integrated teams. Refugio won the game 28–7 on their way to a perfect 10–0 regular season. The Refugio playoff run ended in a loss against Nederland, a high school in a "sundown town" in East Texas near Beaumont. The Refugio players encountered real racism in the

Nederland game. During the week prior to the game, the school received an anonymous letter that among other things said, "Don't bring your niggers because we won't be responsible for their safety," and, "If any nigger scores a touchdown, they will be shot." The racial taunts during the game were vicious.[5]

While the 1955 season was a disaster at Yoakum, the fortunes at Robstown went in the opposite direction. Led by hard-running fullback Willie Jones, who was only a junior, Robstown completed the season with a 6–4 record. Robstown had even more success in 1956. The team defeated Refugio 6–0 in the opener, but then the next week lost to Sinton by the same score. Robstown then reeled off eight consecutive wins to earn the district championship. In the playoffs, Robstown beat Mission 7–0 before losing to San Antonio Edison 20–0, ending the season with a 10–2 record. Willie Jones became the first Black football player in Texas to be named all-state.

Of course, integration affects more than the football team. During the first year of integration, Robstown High was preparing for the annual Senior Ball. Traditionally, this event was held at a nice hotel in Corpus Christi. When school officials called to make reservations, they were asked about integration. Since the school was integrated, they were told by hotel personnel that the Black students would be welcome but would have to enter through the back door. Rather than embarrass these students, the school held the Senior Ball at another location.

Despite exceptional football talents, Willie Jones was totally ignored by White schools in the South during the recruiting process. It would be another decade before a Black player would wear the uniform of a Southwest Conference school. Smaller colleges in the state, such as North Texas and Texas A&I, would integrate before SWC schools, but these schools were still years away from abandoning their segregation policies. Consequently, Jones's choices were limited to going to one of the Black schools in the South or going north. Jones chose to go north and accepted a scholarship at Purdue University. He had a very successful career at Purdue and then played a couple years of professional football with the Buffalo Bills. Jones and Dorothy Cain were married for forty-one years. Willie Jones died on September 9, 2016, at the age of seventy-seven.

A few years later, Robstown would produce other exceptional Black football players—Eugene Upshaw and his younger brother by one year,

Marvin. When playing Little League baseball in the late 1950s, the Upshaw boys led their team to a tournament in Louisville, Kentucky, where they came within one game of going to the Little League World Series. After both starred at Robstown High School, Marvin played college football at Trinity University in San Antonio, while Eugene played at Texas A&I, today known as Texas A&M-Kingsville. Both had very successful professional careers. Eugene, a six-foot-five, 260-pound offensive guard, was the first-round draft choice of the Oakland Raiders, where he played his entire sixteen-year career. He was named all-pro eight times and was a two-time Super Bowl champion. Eugene then became the executive director of the NFL Players Association. Eugene died on August 20, 2008. Marvin played nine years for the Browns, Chiefs, and Cardinals as a defensive lineman.

The Robstown-Yoakum game wasn't the only forfeit that occurred during the first year of integration in Texas. A few weeks later, Rockdale forfeited a game to integrated San Saba. The Black player on the San Saba team had been required to make the long round trip to Brady for school the year before his school integrated. Later that school year, during the spring of 1956, Wharton High forfeited the state championship girls' basketball game to Beeville because Beeville High had a substitute player who was Black.

Brownwood

Several other Black students who attended desegregated schools in the late 1950s and early 1960s had to face the injustices of a segregated society. The West Texas community of Brownwood desegregated its schools as soon as it was legally possible to do so. As mentioned earlier, Brownwood High School integrated in 1955, and by 1960 all Brownwood schools were completely integrated. Although the community's Black population was relatively small, it wasn't long before there were several Black students participating in sports. During the 1955–56 school year, Allen Reed was among the first Black students at Brownwood High and became the school's first Black student athlete. The following year, Black students Willie Cook, Freddie Paul Williams, Harold Reece, and Albert Thompson all participated in Brownwood High athletics. While the Black athletes would participate in home contests, they were often not allowed to travel on the road with the team because of the opposing school's demands or because of concerns about potential harsh treatment.

In 1960, Gordon Wood (May 25, 1914–December 17, 2003) was hired as the head football coach at Brownwood High.[6] Wood, who is White, grew up in West Texas. While his family moved often, they were always near the West Texas city of Abilene. Much of Wood's youth was spent doing farm work, especially picking cotton. As the cotton harvest would stretch throughout the autumn months, Wood often didn't start school until December. This didn't concern his parents much because they put little emphasis on education. Upon completing high school, Wood was offered an athletic scholarship to Hardin-Simmons University in Abilene, primarily because he could run fast. His parents were initially opposed to him attending college, but eventually they gave him their consent since his scholarship covered much of the cost.

While at Hardin-Simmons, Wood decided he would like to be a coach. After college, he got his first job as a teacher and an assistant football coach at Spur, a small town in West Texas. Given the chance, Wood rapidly climbed the coaching ladder. He was soon named the head coach at Stamford High School, a slightly larger small town in West Texas. His desire to learn was legendary. He would drive hours to watch the Texas Tech linebackers practice so he would be better prepared to teach his own linebackers. Baylor Coach Grant Teaff tells how Wood would spend hours learning the details of what made a particular play successful. In 1955 and 1956, Wood's Stamford High teams won back-to-back state championships.

Wood was then hired by Brownwood High, an even larger West Texas school. At Brownwood, Wood brought immediate success as the integrated Brownwood team rolled to the class 3A state championship in 1960, his first year at that job. The team defeated Port Lavaca Calhoun, coached by Bobby Goff, in the championship game. By the time Wood retired following the 1985 season, he had compiled a record of 396–91–15 in forty-three seasons as a head coach, the final twenty-six at Brown-wood. This was the most victories for any football coach in the nation at any level in the twentieth century. Coach Wood won twenty-five district titles and nine state championships, including seven at Brownwood.

Coach Wood told me about several times his integrated teams were exposed to ugly racism in his early days as a football coach. One time Coach Wood helped drive the basketball team to a game in Vernon. The team arrived early and decided to go to a matinee movie to pass the time. Several of the White boys had purchased their tickets and were waiting for the rest of the team in the theater lobby when one of the Black team members reached the front of the line. The theater manager told the Black players they'd have to sit in the balcony if they wanted to see the movie. Upon hearing this, the players who had already purchased tickets got their money refunded, and the entire team decided to find another activity to occupy their time until the game started.

One of the first Black athletes coached by Gordon Wood at Brownwood High was Cecil Houston (September 30, 1944–July 20, 2017). Houston was a descendent of one of the four Black families who came as enslaved people with the first White settlers to Brown County. Houston's older brother, Bennie, was the valedictorian of the last graduating class at Hardin School in Brownwood before integration. Houston told me that he was not aware of major racial problems in the Brownwood schools during his time as a student.[7] He noted, however, that people are a product of their times, and events that were common at the time would not be tolerated today. He and other Black people were accepted in the community if they stayed in their place. Going on the road with an integrated high school team in that era often resulted in extremely uncomfortable situations for the young athletes and their coaches. Houston recalls going with his Brownwood High teammates to Coleman High to play a basketball game. Prior to the start of the game, Coleman High officials approached the Brownwood team and told them that Black players were not allowed at Coleman High. The Black athletes were then escorted to the dressing room, where they changed into street clothes. Once in street clothes, the players were allowed to sit by their teammates on the bench and watch the game. Houston also remembers several occasions when he was not allowed to sit with his teammates in a restaurant but would have to eat in the kitchen. In Houston's view, however, eating in the kitchen was not all that bad. It seems many of the restaurant cooks in those days were Black, and they would take special pride in the Black athletes and take care of them. While the rest of the team was eating hamburgers, Houston was in the kitchen eating steaks. There were other occasions when the Black players were required to wait on the bus during meal stops. Their White teammates then brought food to the Black players on the bus from the restaurant.

Gordon Wood recalls that in 1960 during his first year as head coach at Brownwood High, tickets for the high school football games were sold at a local hardware store. On one occasion, the mother of one of the Black players on his team, Ted Harris, went to purchase a ticket so she could watch her son play. Those selling the tickets, however, refused to let Mrs. Harris buy a ticket. Upon hearing about this, Bernice Wood, Coach Wood's wife, gave a ticket to Mrs. Harris and sat by her during the game. From that day until the end of their lives, Mrs. Wood and Mrs. Harris remained the best of friends.

Coach Wood also recalls that during his early years coaching at Brownwood, the team would always eat at a favorite restaurant when their travels took them to Stephenville. On one trip to Stephenville in the mid-1960s, the Brownwood team had made their orders when the restaurant manager approached the team. He said the Black players were welcome to eat, but they would have to eat in the kitchen. By this time, the team was tired of the unfair treatment of their Black athletes, and so the entire team left the restaurant and didn't return for several years. The restaurant manager later called Coach Wood and apologized. Following the apology, the Brownwood team began returning to the restaurant and continued to do so for many years.

One of the Black players on the Brownwood team during the Stephenville restaurant incident was James Harris, brother of Ted Harris. James Harris went on to play college football and later played for the Washington Redskins (now Commanders) in the NFL. Coach Wood also recalls coaching several other exceptional Black athletes during his tenure at Brownwood. One of the most memorable was Rollin Hunter. In 1967, Hunter became the first Black football recruit at Baylor. Hunter had a fine football career at Baylor, and he also did very well academically.

After tearing down many racial barriers at Brownwood High, Cecil Houston, Ted and James Harris, and other Black athletes were not through blazing new trails. After graduating from Brownwood High, Ted Harris initially attended the all-Black Texas Southern University in Houston. Two years later he transferred to the recently desegregated

Howard Payne University in his hometown of Brownwood. Harris had the honor of being the first Black graduate of Howard Payne. Houston earned a football scholarship to Cisco Junior College, and there became a pioneer in the integration of junior college football in Texas. Cecil Houston's children have also done extremely well. Cecil Houston's oldest daughter, Ramona, was the first Black valedictorian at Brownwood High in 1987 and then earned a doctorate in history from the University of Texas. Another daughter, Rhesa, is a DVM (Doctor of Veterinary Medicine) in Birmingham, Alabama. Dr. Ramona Houston told me that while Brownwood schools desegregated early and were ahead of many schools in other parts of the state on racial issues, there were still problems. For example, it was not until the 1980s that Brownwood High had a Black cheerleader.[8]

Dimmit

The first decade of school integration in Texas was also the time when an exceptional Black athlete, Junior Coffey (March 21, 1942–August 30, 2021), emerged from the tiny Texas Panhandle community of Dimmit.[9] Prior to integration, only a handful of Black families lived in the Dimmit area. The children of these Black families met in an old run-down building where they were taught by a single teacher. At one time this teacher was Beral Hance (September 25, 1913–December 8, 2000), a White woman and mother of Kent Hance, born November 14, 1942, a future US congressman and chancellor of the Texas Tech University System. Residents from the 1950s remember how Mrs. Hance would often stop and buy groceries on her way to school. Mrs. Hance stated that many times the kids would come to school hungry, and they couldn't learn until they had eaten.[10]

Dimmit schools integrated soon after the *Brown* Supreme Court decision. One of the Black students in the early years of integration was Junior Coffey. Coffey was the star running back on the football team and an outstanding basketball player. During both his junior and senior years (1960 and 1961), Coffey led his team to the Class 2A state basketball championship game in Austin. While Dimmit lost both championship games, Coffey was the first Black player to play in the state basketball tournament in Austin.

By being a Black person in a virtually White world, Coffey and his Dimmit teammates often experienced the brunt of a segregated society. Coffey and some of his former teammates describe how Coffey was sometimes shielded from some racial bigotry. As the team was traveling to and from games on the school bus and it came time to eat, Kent Hance would go into the restaurant to reportedly see if they were willing to serve an entire football or basketball team. Coffey told me that it was several years later when he learned that in reality, Hance was asking if they would serve a Black person. Despite these precautions, they still came face-to-face with racial prejudice on several occasions. Once a waitress seated them in an obscure corner of the restaurant and then closed some venetian blinds so they would be out of sight of the rest of the restaurant's patrons. On another occasion, after the team was in the restaurant, the manager came and said that Black boy was welcome to eat in the restaurant, but he would have to eat in the kitchen. At this point, the entire team returned to the bus and sought another eating establishment. While in Austin for the state basketball tournament, the team was forced to stay in a roach-infested outpost because Coffey was not allowed to stay in the segregated Austin hotels, and the team insisted on all staying together.[11]

While on the basketball court or the football field, Coffey experienced the usual racial taunts of the era. Despite these obstacles, Coffey developed into a high school athlete who was known nationally, and college recruiters from all over the country sought his services. His first choice was the University of Texas, but the Longhorns would not integrate for years. The nearby Texas Tech Red Raiders had recently joined the Southwest Conference and showed some initial interest, but then backed off. Obviously rejected by Southwest Conference schools, Coffey then seriously considered going to the University of Oklahoma from the Big Eight Conference as the Sooner football team had recently integrated. Coffey admits that part of the reasons he considered Oklahoma was that it provided him a chance to even the score with Longhorns when the two schools met in the Cotton Bowl on the second Saturday of October each year. Coffey, however, eventually decided to leave Texas and go to the University of Washington in Seattle. Jim Owens, the Washington head coach at the time, was an assistant coach at Texas A&M under Bear Bryant before taking the Washington job in 1956. Most likely, while at A&M Owens made contacts in Texas that helped make him aware of high school players and helped him recruit the state. Coffey pushed the Huskies to two Rose Bowl appearances and left as the program's second leading all time rusher. Coffey then played seven years in the NFL with Green Bay, Atlanta, and the New York Giants before a knee injury shortened his career. He was a member of some of the great Vince Lombardi-coached Packer teams of the 1960s, including some that won NFL championships before there was a Super Bowl.

South Texas Cities: San Antonio and Corpus Christi

These pioneering standouts at Robstown, Brownwood, and Dimmit all thrived at schools that, for the most part, fully complied with the Brown ruling. They encountered some common obstacles, such as isolation and marginalization at overwhelmingly White schools and incidents of blatant racism on road trips to still segregated communities. On the other hand, they were among the few Black student athletes of that era who—as a result of being integrated into overwhelmingly White schools—had access to better funded programs and received more media coverage and publicity.

The Black student athletes in the two largest cities of South Texas, San Antonio and Corpus Christi, faced a different set of challenges. Both school districts moved to integrate shortly after the *Brown* ruling. In practice, however, that integration was largely tokenism. In 1955 it was not only San Antonio's schools, but also its neighborhoods that were strictly segregated. Public policies and private mortgage lending standards enforced "redlining" that made it virtually impossible for Black or Hispanic residents to own property in the northern part of the city. Wheatley High School, located in the city's predominantly Black east side was an officially segregated Black school, while schools in several west and east San Antonio neighborhoods were nearly exclusively Hispanic. After integration was announced in 1955, the redlining of the city's neighborhoods largely preserved the de facto segregation of the schools, and little changed for most students.

One of the few previously segregated White schools that did experience an influx of minority students was Brackenridge High School, a school in central San Antonio surrounded by Black and Hispanic neighborhoods.

Against this complicated backdrop, no one made a greater impression than Warren McVea. Despite being only five foot eight and 170 pounds, McVea was one of the most feared running backs in the history of Texas high school football. McVea had blinding speed, cat-like quickness, tremendous ability to change directions, and was almost impossible to tackle in the open field. McVea first gained statewide notoriety during the fall of 1962, his junior year. Brackenridge had made it to the playoffs despite three losses and was an underdog in each of the play-off games it played. After three upset wins, Brackenridge had made it to the state semifinals and were scheduled to play undefeated and top-ranked Spring Branch of Houston. Along the line of scrimmage, the Brackenridge players were outweighed by about fifty pounds per person. In one of the biggest upsets in Texas high school football history, Brackenridge beat Spring Branch 30–23. Warren McVea scored two touchdowns and quarterback Victor Castillo passed for 368 yards. Prior to this game, Spring Branch had only given up 37 points all year. This put McVea and the Eagles in the championship game against highly regarded Borger, a powerhouse from the Texas Panhandle. Following the state championship game, the *Dallas Morning News* reported, "The skinny-legged Brackenridge Eagles rode the passing arm of little Victor Castillo and the flying feet of slippery Warren McVea to an upset 30–26 victory over Borger for the Texas schoolboy Class AAAA football championship."[12]

After leading his team to the state championship in 1962, McVea was one of the most highly regarded athletes in the state going into his senior year. McVea did not disappoint as he led his team to win after win. On November 15, 1963, Brackenridge rapped up the District 16 4A title with a 54–0 win over intracity rival McCollum. During the game, McVea scored six touchdowns, and the thirty-six points gave him the all-time city career scoring record. The Eagles first playoff game was against Robert E. Lee High of San Antonio, the undefeated and all-White champions of District 15 4A, who were led by all-state back Linus Baer. Baer would go on to play college football at the University of Texas.

In the 1984 issue of Dave Campbell's *Texas Football*, the game between Lee and Brackenridge held in San Antonio on November 29, 1963—one week after President John F. Kennedy was shot in Dallas—was voted as the best high school football game in the state during the magazines first twenty-five years of existence. An element of intrigue was added by the fact that Lee was that an all-White team playing against an integrated Brackenridge team. There was not a single punt the entire game. Only the halftime clock and a fumble prevented Brackenridge from scoring every time they had the ball. The sensational Warren McVea scored six touchdowns, while rushing for 215 yards on twenty-one attempts. The score was tied when Lee scored with eighteen seconds left to take a 55–48 lead. After Brackenridge failed on two desperate attempts to get McVea open during the final seconds, the game ended with Lee hanging on for the dramatic win.[13]

Following McVea's high school career, a major national recruiting battle ensued as colleges all over the country tried to convince him to enroll with them. The University of Missouri even got former President Harry Truman to assist in their recruiting efforts. Still noticeable for their lack of effort to recruit McVea were the schools of the Southwest Conference. McVea eventually accepted a scholarship from the University of Houston and Coach Bill Yeoman, becoming the first Black football player at that school. At the time, Houston was not yet a member of the Southwest Conference. While at the University of Houston, McVea's career had moments of brilliance. He was the first Black athlete to ever play against Ole Miss, Mississippi State, Kentucky, Tennessee, Miami, and Florida State. During his sophomore season, he caught six passes for a school record 201 yards in an upset win against Ole Miss. In the Ole Miss game, he had touchdown receptions of eighty and eighty-four yards. During his junior year, McVea had a ninety-nine-yard touchdown reception, and he averaged 8.8 yards per carry from scrimmage and 27.6 yards per pass reception. As a senior, McVea led the Cougars to a number two national ranking at one point. An injury then slowed McVea, and the Cougars lost three games. He then went on to play five years of professional football.

As with San Antonio, the South Texas city of Corpus Christi announced it would integrate its schools soon after it was legally possible to do so. The city was mostly Hispanic and White, and the relatively small Black population attended the segregated Solomon Coles High School. The school was named for a former enslaved person who learned to read in violation of the law at the time and eventually earned a bachelor's degree in divinity from Yale, among other degrees. Coles then came to Corpus Christi and founded the school named in his honor in 1893.

Solomon Coles, located in the city's predominantly Black neighborhoods on the north side of the city remained open after integration began
in 1954, but Black students could choose to attend one of the city's White
schools. During the late 1950s, several talented Black athletes chose to
attend the formerly all-White Miller High School, located five miles to
the west. One such person was LeFord Fant, who went from Miller High
to become the first Black football player at Texas Western, now called the
University of Texas at El Paso. Following in his footsteps in 1958, Bobby
Smith played for Miller High and became the first Black person to be
named to the all-state football team in the largest school classification.
He then played for North Texas State (now University of North Texas),
and later for the Buffalo Bills. In 1960, led by talented running back
Johnny Roland, Miller became the first integrated Texas high school
team to win a state UIL football championship. Roland played college
football at Missouri, where he was the team's first Black captain. He then
had a successful pro career.

Art Delgado (born December 18, 1941), who played at Miller during
this era and later played for Baylor, remembers there were good relation-
ships among the Black, White, and Hispanic members of that team.[14]
There were, however, problems off the field. In 1958, when Delgado was
a sophomore, the Miller football team traveled to Wichita Falls and
were greeted by signs with messages such as, "Nigger go back to Africa."
When they returned to their bus following the game, they found that all
the windows had been broken out. The 1960 state championship game
between Miller and the same Wichita Falls team was held in Baylor
Stadium in Waco. The Miller team was forced to stay in Temple, about
thirty miles away because there were no desegregated hotels in Waco.
Miller won the game by a score of 13–6. The championship Miller team
had eighteen White players, seventeen Latino players, and six Black
players.

PVIL Football

While Warren McVea, Willie Jones, Junior Coffey, Johnny Roland,
and a few other Black high school athletes in Texas benefited from the
advantages of playing with and against mostly White players on mostly
well-funded teams, the vast majority of Black high school athletes con-

tinued to play in the anonymity of the PVIL during the first decade of school integration in Texas. While the UIL accepted schools with Black athletes, the formerly segregated Black schools continued to participate in the Prairie View League until 1966, as will be discussed later. During the late 1950s and early 1960s, sports sections in the major city papers were filled with information and stories about high school football. In September, predictions about the likely order of finish in each district filled the papers. By the time December rolled around, large headlines and long stories described the playoffs. One looks in vain, however, for information regarding the hundreds of Black high schools that were still not recognized by the UIL.

In 1959, for example, the *San Antonio Express* provided extensive coverage of all the UIL schools in the city, most of which had integrated teams. However, the Black high school in the city, Wheatley, was never mentioned. The 1959 San Antonio all-city team included one Black person—Clifford Stallings, a six-foot-two, 185-pound senior back who played for the Brackenridge Eagles. Meanwhile, the Black players on the Wheatley team remained anonymous. When December rolled around, the football playoffs in all four UIL classifications received extensive coverage, while participants in the PVIL playoffs are now a mystery. In a rare entry on Wednesday, December 16, 1959, the *Dallas Morning News* reported that Dallas Lincoln would play Beaumont Hebert the following Saturday for the "State Negro High School Championship." The following Sunday, the paper simply reported that Hebert had won the game 37–0. The paper provided no descriptions of the events or the star players.[15]

Many people who followed high school football in the pre-integration days tended to ridicule PVIL football. It was reported to be unstructured and loosey-goosey; the players were supposedly weak in fundamentals and mechanics. Such views were especially popular among coaches and administrators of the Southwest Conference and other southern colleges, which justified their not recruiting Black players. Anyone, however, who harbored such views had probably never watched a game between two good Black high school football teams. Looking at the evidence from a later perspective, there is little doubt that there were teams playing PVIL football that could have competed against any high school in the state. In fact, the 1959 Beaumont Hebert state championship team just mentioned may have been one of the best high school football teams ever to play in the state of Texas at any level or under any classification.

There is little question that during the years of PVIL football, many of the best teams emerged from the Golden Triangle area of Beaumont, Port Arthur, and Orange in Southeast Texas. To provide an indication of the quality of football played in this area, where the population about 130,000 at the time, there were twenty-seven Beaumont natives playing NFL football in 1973, and most of these players were Black.[16] Segregation was much more firmly entrenched in Beaumont, an industrial city split roughly equally between Black and White residents, than in Texas communities in the south and west. The city's schools remained in strict defiance of the Supreme Court's ruling in the first decade following the *Brown* decision. Many of the exceptional Black players that emerged from the area learned to play football in Liberia Park on the south side of Beaumont. It was there that hundreds of kids spent their free hours playing football games that continued evening after evening, almost without end. For many of these kids, professional football was the great American dream, their hope of escaping poverty and discrimination.[17]

When these young Black kids reached high school, their dream of making it big in football continued. In those days, there were two Black high schools in Beaumont, Hebert and Charlton-Pollard. During the final years of segregation, both schools were led by legendary coaches: Charlton-Pollar by Willie Ray Smith Sr. (April 11, 1911–January 3, 1992)[18] and Hebert by Clifton Ozen (June 30, 1923–February 13, 1995.)[19] The Beaumont district later named schools in honor of both coaches. Ozen was hired by the South Park School District in Beaumont to be a history teacher and an assistant coach in 1948. In 1959, he became the head coach at Hebert High School. During his coaching career, he won 110 games while losing only twenty-eight and tying four. He also won two state championships.

When Ozen took over the Hebert team in 1959, he inherited a team loaded with talent. Among the players on the 1959 Hebert team were Mel Farr, Miller Farr, Anthony Guillory, and Warren Wells. The Hebert team rolled through the season undefeated, and crushed Dallas Lincoln in the state championship game 37–0. The 1959 all-Black team from Hebert High in Beaumont was, without question, one of the most talented high school football teams ever. Yet this team played in virtual anonymity.

The talent level of the team is evident from the subsequent careers of some of the more prominent players. Following high school, Miller Farr starred as a college defensive back for Wichita State. He later played pro football for the St. Louis Cardinals and the Houston Oilers. Miller's younger brother Mel was the "slowest" member of a talented backfield, running a one hundred-yard dash in 9.8 seconds. After high school, Mel had over seventy-five scholarship offers, none of which came from Southwest Conference schools. He attended UCLA and starred as a halfback, earning first-team all-American recognition in 1966. Mel Farr then had a productive NFL career with the Detroit Lions. Anthony Guillory played college football for Nebraska, and later played as a linebacker with the Los Angeles Rams of the NFL. Warren Wells chose to stay in Texas to play his college football and enrolled at the all-Black Texas Southern. He later played in the NFL as a wide receiver for the Detroit Lions and Oakland Raiders. While with the Raiders he scored many touchdowns on passes thrown by Kenny Stabler, including one in the 1970 AFC Championship game against the Baltimore Colts. Former Raider coach John Madden described Wells as one of the best athletes he ever coached.

Even after the super talented team of 1959 had graduated, Hebert High continued to produce outstanding football players. Perhaps the best known was Jerry LeVias, a cousin of Miller and Mel Farr. While relatively small, LeVias had the speed and quickness to put fear into the hearts of opponents every time he touched the ball. The first time he touched the football as a ninth-grader in a varsity game at Hebert, LeVias ran sixty-five yards for a touchdown. During his junior and senior seasons, LeVias averaged forty-five yards on kickoff returns and 10.8 yards per carry from scrimmage, and he scored forty-three touchdowns. LeVias would become the first Black player to receive a football scholarship from a Southwest Conference school when he attended SMU.

Beaumont's other Black high school, Charlton-Pollard also produced its share of exceptional football players, including one of the most imposing figures to ever step onto a high school football field in Texas or anywhere else—Bubba Smith. Bubba was the son of Charlton-Pollard head coach Willie Ray Smith Sr. The six-foot-eight Smith could dominate a game like few others. When it came time for Bubba Smith to choose a college, the Southwest Conference schools were not interested. Smith enrolled at Michigan State, and during his senior year he led the Spartans to an undefeated season. The only blemish on the Spartans' record that year was a 10–10 tie with Notre Dame in a game that featured two undefeated teams ranked number one and number two in the country. Smith was first-team all-American in 1966 and was the first player selected in the 1967 NFL draft. He became an all-pro football player and then a well-known TV personality and movie star. He is perhaps best known for his role in the *Police Academy* movies.

Bubba's two brothers also played for Charlton-Pollard. Willie Ray Smith Jr. was a six-foot, 190-pound running back who played college football at Kansas with Gale Sayers. Smith Sr. considered Willie Ray Jr. the best player he ever coached, but a knee injury during his senior year at Kansas ruined a promising pro career. Tody Smith, a six-foot-five defensive end also had an outstanding career at Charlton-Pollard and followed his brother Bubba to Michigan State. He later transferred to USC and played in the NFL for the Cowboys, Oilers, and Bills.

There were other exceptionally talented Black Texas athletes who played football in the forgotten era of the PVIL. One of these was Kenny Houston of Lufkin. Like Beaumont, the East Texas town of Lufkin retained strict school segregation following *Brown*, with Black students, including Houston, attending PVIL-affiliated Dunbar High School. After a successful high school career, Houston decided to remain in Texas for college and accepted a scholarship to Prairie View. He was instrumental in leading Prairie View to a small college national championship in 1963. Houston then went on to an extremely successful pro football career as a defensive back. He played six years for the Houston Oilers and eight years for the Washington Redskins (now Commanders) and was selected to play in the Pro Bowl ten times. He led the AFL with nine interceptions in 1971 and had forty-nine interceptions for his career. In 1986 he was voted into the Pro Football Hall of Fame. After his playing days, Houston became an assistant coach with the University of Houston.

A number of others who played high school in the PVIL later made a name for themselves in pro football. These individuals include NFL Hall of Famer Charlie Taylor, who attended the all-Black Dalworth High in Grand Prairie. Taylor went to college at Arizona State, and later caught 649 passes while playing for the Washington Redskins (now Commanders). For a while, Taylor was the NFL's all-time leading pass receiver. Otis Taylor was a quarterback at Houston Worthing before going to Prairie View. At Prairie View he teamed with Kenny Houston in leading the school to the 1963 national championship. Later, as a receiver for the Kansas City Chiefs, he caught 410 passes for 7,306 yards and fifty-seven touchdowns. Dick "Night Train" Lane was rescued from a garbage dumpster as an infant by Emma Lane, who then raised him as her own son. He had been left in the dumpster by his prostitute mother.[20] He grew up and attended PVIL-affiliated Anderson High in Austin. In the NFL, he once held the record for career interceptions with sixty-eight. He remains perhaps the most feared defensive back in NFL history. His clothesline tackles were so vicious that they were later outlawed by the league. "Mean" Joe Greene played at Temple Dunbar before attending North Texas State (now the University of North Texas). He was an all-American in 1968 before joining the Pittsburgh Steelers and being an integral part of the famed Steel Curtain defense that helped the Steelers win four Super Bowls during the 1970s. Cedric Hardman played high school football at Aldine Carver. He was teammates with Joe Greene at North Texas and then played thirteen years in the NFL. Gene Washington grew up in La Porte, but attended high school at Baytown Carver, because La Porte didn't have a school for Black students. Washington was a talented sprinter who attended Michigan State with Bubba Smith. He was an all-American in 1966 and had a successful pro career with the Minnesota Vikings. Many, many others could be named, but the point that the PVIL produced many outstanding players and teams in the pre-integration era is obvious.

An examination of the 1967 professional football draft provides an indication of the quality of PVIL football. Following the 1966 season, the established NFL and the upstart AFL came to an agreement in which the champion of each league would meet at the end of season in what became Super Bowl I. The two leagues also agreed to hold a joint draft to avoid bidding wars for top players. The first Super Bowl, played in Los Angeles on January 15, 1967, pitted the NFL champion Green Bay Packers against the AFL champion Kansas City Chiefs. The Chiefs had six players who had played PVIL high school football in Texas. In the first-ever joint NFL/AFL draft, three of the first eight players taken had played PVIL football in Texas. The first pick was Bubba Smith of Beaumont Charlton-Pollard; the seventh pick was Mel Farr of Beaumont Hebert; and the eighth pick was Gene Washington from Baytown Carver.[21]

There are also many examples of great Black athletes whose opportunities were limited by simple racial prejudice. Many people who watched Eldridge Dickey play consider him to be one of the most talented quarterbacks they had ever seen. Dickey played high school football at the all-Black Booker T. Washington High in Houston. He then attended college at Tennessee State where he was a three-time Black college all-American and led his team to an undefeated Black-college national championship season. Prior to the 1968 pro football draft, one observer noted that if Eldridge Dickey was White, twenty-six pro teams would be chasing him.[22] The Oakland Raiders, under the ownership of Al Davis, selected Dickey in the first round of the draft and Kenny Stabler from Alabama in the second round. During his first preseason, Dickey played very well at quarterback, but was still moved to wide receiver when the regular season began. Not even the maverick Al Davis was willing to play a Black quarterback in the 1960s. Kenny Stabler then became the team's starting quarterback for many years.

Hank Stram, head coach of the Kansas City Chiefs, later stated, "What happened to Eldridge Dickey has to go down in history as one of the greatest sports crimes ever committed. The entire sports world and Eldridge Dickey was robbed by the Oakland Raiders in 1968. During the preseason, he outperformed nearly every quarterback in the AFC and NFC. . . . Dickey was special and just too talented. He was fast, he had a powerful arm and could throw with both hands. He was truly one of the most accurate passers I've ever seen. I wanted him badly, but Oakland selected him first."[23] Dickey never got a chance to take a snap as quarterback in a regular season NFL game and died in 2000 at the age of fifty-four.

Chapter Five

Texas High School Football Integration, 1964–1970

In the first two decades following *Brown v. Board of Education*, national awareness of and sympathy toward the plight of Blacks in the South and elsewhere increased greatly. By the early 1960s, a full-blown social movement had emerged—the civil rights movement. Factors important in the rise of the civil rights movement in the early 1960s included the supportive Kennedy and later Johnson administrations in Washington and charismatic leaders such as Martin Luther King Jr. Significant policies, including the Civil Rights Act of 1964 and the Voting Rights Act of 1965, provided a legal framework to end discriminatory policies. Significantly, schools had to meet federal desegregation standards to receive federal funds.

In the mid-1960s, critical events occurred that received widespread media coverage and brought the cruelty of racism and segregation into the homes of people throughout the country. These included police brutality against civil rights protesters on Edmund Pettus Bridge in Alabama and the murder of three civil rights workers in Neshoba County, Mississippi. Later in the decade, major race riots impacted cities throughout the country. To help understand the racial unrest, President Johnson established the Kerner Commission. In March 1968, the commission released its report, which stated, "Our nation is moving toward two societies, one white, one black, separate and unequal." The report then clearly stated that the tinder for the racial unrest was White racism. It claimed, "White society is deeply implicated in the ghetto. White institutions created it, white institutions maintain it, and white society condones it."[1]

By the mid-1960s, the "White only" signs were coming down, and whether people liked it or not, the "old South" was coming to an end. Under these conditions, it was nearly impossible for southern school districts to publicly maintain a policy of complete segregation. Consequently, virtually every school district in the state of Texas and throughout the South formally announced that they were desegregated. When faced with a decision of whether to desegregate or lose federal funds, the schools opted to desegregate.

In reality, many school districts were simply changing tactics from outright defiance to token compliance, and therefore the number of Black students actually attending schools with White students did not greatly increase. So long as housing remained largely segregated, maintaining de facto school segregation was easy. More clever means of keeping the races separate in schools emerged. One of the more common plans was the so-called freedom of choice. Under this approach, a school district would announce that it was desegregated but would keep open both the former all-Black school and the former all-White school. Students were then allowed the freedom to choose which school in the district they would attend. Not surprisingly, virtually all the Black students continued to attend the formerly Black schools and nearly all the White students continued to attend the formerly White schools. There were several reasons for this, not the least of which were severe social pressure and the discrimination a student would face in a school if he or she were a part of a small racial minority. In addition, housing remained heavily segregated in many American cities after decades of redlining and other discriminatory housing policies. Often the White schools were located in the White part of town, while Black schools were located in overwhelmingly Black neighborhoods. Additionally, most White students preferred the White schools, which typically had better facilities and equipment. For a Black student to choose to attend the White school, it would mean time-consuming and expensive commuting, as well as being socially marginalized and isolated from friends and familiar teachers. These freedom of choice plans thus technically complied with desegregation standards while in practice admitting only a token handful of Black students.

Jerry Honore grew up in Lake Charles, Louisiana, but his experience with the freedom of choice approach to desegregation was similar to what students throughout Texas and the South encountered. In 1968, the Lake Charles School District announced that its schools were officially desegregated. However, the school district kept both the former White school (Lake Charles High) and the former Black high school (W. O. Boston High) open. Not surprisingly, none of the White students chose to attend W. O. Boston, and Honore was one of only a handful of Black students who chose to attend Lake Charles High. Honore was the only Black member of the Lake Charles High football team. He told me that he experienced discrimination on a somewhat regular basis but chose to stay at the school. Harsh treatment also occurred on the field during football games. His efforts were rewarded when he became the first Black scholarship football player at Texas A&M University.[2]

Gerrymandered school district boundaries often hardened the freedom of choice approach for maintaining de facto segregation. Often even relatively small communities would have two or more separate school districts, and the boundaries between the districts would be drawn so that most of the White students would live in one district, while most of the Black students would live in another. Freedom of choice policies resulted in enhanced segregation as those White students who lived within the boundaries of the primarily Black school district could—and often did—transfer into the White district and vice-versa.

Even as outright defiance of school desegregation faded in the 1960s, the racial aspects of Texas high school football remained relatively constant through the midsixties. That is, a vast majority of the participants in UIL sponsored activities were White, while nearly all Black high school athletes continued to participate in the Prairie View League. Then in 1966, rapid change began. In that year, Wheatley High School, the all-Black San Antonio school, petitioned to be admitted to the UIL, and its petition was granted. So, for the first time, an all-Black former PVIL school was participating in the UIL. That year, the San Antonio Wheatley High football team had a 6–3–1 record and finished in a tie for second place in their district.

The following year, 1967, numerous other Black schools followed the Wheatley example and jumped from the Prairie View League to the UIL. The movement of Black schools to the UIL meant the end of the Prairie View League and it soon disbanded.[3] The end of the Prairie View League was not without drawbacks. For example, some of the most storied high school rivalries in the country were curtailed by UIL regulations. One such rivalry was between Yates High in Houston and Wheatley High of Houston, which was named, like its San Antonio counterpart, after Phillis Wheatley, an early African American poet. The November 23, 1966, *Houston Post* stated, "When the Wheatley Wildcats and the Yates Lions clash on Thanksgiving Day, it will mark the end of an era. The nationally famous Thanksgiving Day dual between the Northside and Third Ward had been played on Thanksgiving every year since 1927. Life Magazine has called it 'the largest regularly scheduled football game in the world.'"[4] When the two schools joined the UIL in 1967, they had to abide by UIL rules that said that district games had to be completed prior to mid-November because of the upcoming playoffs. As a result, they could no longer play on Thanksgiving. A crowd of 28,121 spectators attended Jeppeson Stadium on the University of Houston campus for the teams' Thanksgiving Day finale in 1966 as Yates defeated Wheatley 6–3. This loss cost Wheatley the district championship and gave the title to Kashmere. With the move away from the traditional Thanksgiving date and the loss of the associated pageantry, the event fade from a center piece of Black culture in Houston into relative obscurity. Similarly, entrance into the UIL changed the classic rivalry between Hebert High and Charlton-Pollard High in Beaumont, a matchup traditionally known as the "Soul Bowl."

In the final Prairie View League Class 4A State Championship game held on December 10, 1966, Beaumont Hebert defeated Dallas Madison 14–3. One of the top performers in this final year of the Prairie View League was Cliff Branch of Houston Worthing. Branch was a world class sprinter and went on to become a star receiver at the University of Colorado. He then played for the Oakland Raiders of the NFL and earned a place in the NFL Hall of Fame.

Thus, when the 1967 school year began, Black and White students were, for the most part, still attending separate schools. However, for the first time the predominantly Black schools and the predominantly White schools would be competing against one another on the football field. The teams from the Black schools entering the UIL for the first time were not expected to do very well against the White schools, according to the preseason polls. For example, the 1967 issue of Dave Campbell's *Texas Football* picked Yates High to finish dead last in their ten-team district

(Zone 1) which included a number of White schools. This is after Yates had won nine district titles during the previous twenty-five years, and in the 1960s had already won the Prairie View League state championship twice. Similarly, Kashmere, which had been district champion in the Houston area's Prairie View League in 1966, was picked to finish seventh in 1967 in Zone 2. In a five-team district in the Beaumont area, defending Prairie View League state champion Hebert was picked fourth, ahead of only Charlton-Pollard, the other Black school in the district.[5]

As the time approached for the first-ever high school football games between predominantly Black former PVIL schools and predominately White UIL schools, coaches and players on both sides began to feel a great deal of tension. To many it felt as though they were not only representing their schools but were carrying the weight of their entire races on their shoulders. Over the years, individual Black players had proven they could compete with Whites, but now entire Black teams, with Black coaching staffs, representing schools with Black teachers and administrators, would be competing against White schools. Luther Booker (August 19, 1928–July 25, 1994), the tremendously successful coach at Yates High, was an assistant coach at Booker T. Washington High School in Houston's Fourth Ward during 1967. He told me that he remembered going into those first games against the White schools convinced that his team had virtually no chance of winning. Booker had heard again and again that the Black teams were not fundamentally sound and were not as well coached as the White teams. After hearing it so many times, he had begun to believe it.[6] Clifton Ozen of Beaumont Hebert expressed similar concerns to me, and both men recalled that their school administrators had a great fear of being blown out and thoroughly embarrassed.[7]

On the other hand, coaches at the White schools had worries of their own. Paul Register (May 26, 1929–May 2, 2007) was a long-time assistant coach at Texas A&M University, but in the 1960s he was an assistant coach and then head football coach at Spring Branch High School in Houston. His team had lost to Brackenridge and Warren McVea in the state semifinals in 1962, and in 1966 his team had lost the state championship game to an integrated San Angelo High team, coached by future Texas A&M Head Coach Emory Bellard (who was also the inventor of the wish bone offense). Register told me that he had watched the Black teams on many occasions and had tremendous fear and respect for their talent.[8]

Once the games began, however, the quality of football being played at the former PVIL schools immediately became evident. On September 14, 1967, in the first district game in Houston between former Prairie View League schools and UIL schools, Yates (a Black school) defeated Westbury (a White school) 26–7. In Houston's Zone 1, Bellaire (a White school) finished with an 8–1 record, which was one game better than Yates and Wheatley (Black schools), which both finished at 7–2. In the other part of the city (Zone 2), Kashmere (a Black school) rolled undefeated through its district games. On October 12, 1967, Kashmere met Sam Houston in a game that would eventually determine the Zone 2 district championship at Delmar Stadium in Houston. Kashmere was victorious in this game 14–6. Several fights broke out in the stands during the game. D. W. Rutledge played in the game for Sam Houston, and later became a legendary head football coach at Converse Judson. He was thoroughly impressed by the Kashmere team. In the city's championship game, more than 28,500 fans crowded into Jeppesen Stadium at the University of Houston and watched Bellaire defeat Kashmere 14–0. This game was especially intriguing because it featured a completely White team against a completely Black team playing for the city championship.

In Beaumont, Hebert and Charlton-Pollard combined to go 6–0 against the three White schools in the city. Then in a classic season-ending matchup, Hebert beat Charlton-Pollard 8–7 to win the district championship. Hebert then beat the champion of the Port Arthur portion of their district, and then Hebert beat Texas City in a bi-district game 42–21. Hebert eventually lost to Houston Bellaire in the state quarterfinals 28–6. Bellaire lost the following week to eventual state champion Austin Reagan in the state semifinals. The state championship in the first year of integration of Texas high school football ended up being a matchup of two all-White schools, a memorable game as Austin Reagan defeated Abilene Cooper 20–19. Cooper was at the Reagan one-yard line when the game ended. Many witnesses swear that Cooper made it into the end zone on the final play of the game. The officials, however, ruled the ball carrier was stopped just short of the goal line. Cooper was led that year by quarterback Jack Mildren. Mildren later went to Oklahoma and led the Sooners to a near national championship in 1971.

The 1967 Texas high school football season had shown beyond any doubt that football games played between the White and Black schools were generally very competitive. In Houston, the Black schools won a majority of the games played between the Black and White schools, and several Black schools progressed deeply into the playoffs. Although the state championship game was between two all-White schools, the Black schools proved to themselves and the world that they could compete. Booker and Ozen both recalled the feeling of relief when they realized that they were as capable as the people on the other side of the field.

Those Friday night gridiron battles in 1967, however, did far more than show that Black high schools could compete with White high schools on the football field. For many, including players, students, school administrators, parents, and fans, these football games forced more contact with members of another race than many had ever experienced before. Many people later shared with me that they knew of people who had deep feelings of prejudice going into the 1967 season. Such contact, no doubt, caused many stereotypes to crumble. The extreme separation of the races that had existed prior to this time had allowed stereotypes to emerge where an individual would be assumed to have certain characteristics simply because of his or her race. Exposure to and awareness of individual differences usually shatters stereotypes.

For the remaining few years of the 1960s, there was relatively little change in the racial composition of Texas high school football. In many East Texas school districts, tokenism remained the norm. While schools claimed to be integrated, the vast majority of Black students were still attending schools that were nearly all Black, while the vast majority of White students were attending schools that were nearly all White. But at least, they were competing against one another on the football field.

In 1968, a number of all-Black schools won district championships among the state's largest schools. These included Booker T. Washington High in Houston, Charlton-Pollard in Beaumont, and Wheatley in San Antonio. Washington made it to the state semifinals, where they lost to Austin Reagan, who went on to repeat as state champions. In Class 2A, Dunbar High School in the East Texas town of Lufkin, which remained nearly completely segregated until 1971, made it to the state finals where they lost 7–6 to Daingerfield. The next year several more Black schools had very successful seasons. District winners among the state's largest schools included Kashmere and Yates from Houston, Beaumont Hebert, and San Antonio Wheatley. Hebert made it to the state semifinals before losing to San Antonio Lee. In 2A, Lufkin Dunbar had another strong team and advanced to the state semifinals against Klein. The game ended in a 23–23 tie, but Klein advanced because of a 17–13 first down advantage.

Opportunities in College Football

College opportunities for Black athletes mirrored the uneven progress that was occurring in high school athletics. As at the high school level, the opening was slow and uneven but began to accelerate in the late 1960s as a few Black athletes were admitted to previously all-White southern college athletic programs. Many of the major programs in the North and the West, in contrast, had recruited a handful of Black athletes going back several decades. Border states began the desegregation process before states in the deep South. In Texas, breakthroughs first occurred at smaller Texas colleges and universities. In 1957, Abner Haynes began playing varsity football at North Texas State (now the University of North Texas) in Denton. Although he was the star of the team, Haynes was not allowed to stay in the same dorm as his teammates and was forced to live with relatives in the Black section of Denton. Haynes was the constant target of verbal and physical abuse, and Ole Miss, Mississippi State, and Chattanooga all canceled scheduled games with North Texas because of Haynes. After playing for North Texas, Haynes joined the Dallas Texans of the newly formed American Football League. During his rookie year, he led the AFL in rushing and was named Rookie of the Year. He stayed with the team as they moved to Kansas City and became the Chiefs.[9]

A year later, in 1958, Prentice Gautt became the first Black football player at the University of Oklahoma. Sid Blanks became an NAIA all-American while playing at Texas A&I (now Texas A&M University Kingsville) and helped the Javelina's win a national championship in 1962. "Pistol" Pete Pedro was the first Black player at West Texas State (now West Texas A&M) and paved the way for other star running backs at the school including Eugene "Mercury" Morris and Duane Thomas. Morris played in three Super Bowls for the Miami Dolphins and was named to the Pro Bowl three times. Thomas played professional football for the Dallas Cowboys and the Washington Redskins (now Commanders).

Some of the larger universities in the South began dipping their toes into the integration waters in the mid-1960s. In 1966, John Westbrook—a walk-on at Baylor from Booker T. Washington High in Elgin—played in Baylor's first game against Syracuse to become the first Black player in a football game for a Southwest Conference team. A week later, SMU opened its season with Jerry LeVias from Beaumont Hebert, who was the first Black athlete to receive a football scholarship to a Southwest Conference school. SMU was picked to finish last in the conference, but with LeVias leading the way the Mustangs won the conference championship and earned the right to play in the Cotton Bowl on January 1, 1967. Midway through his second year at SMU, LeVias had already broken the school's all-time pass receiving record. During his senior year, LeVias led the nation in the number of passes caught and finished fifth in Heisman Trophy voting. He often experienced harsh treatment and even received death threats while playing football at SMU. On one occasion, the school received a letter saying LeVias would be shot if he played. LeVias played anyway. His teammates stood around him while the team huddled to provide protection. The spring following his senior year, LeVias graduated with honors from SMU.[10]

In 1968, walk-ons J. T. Reynolds and Sammy Williams played sparingly for Texas A&M. A year later, walk-on Hugh McElroy joined the team. In 1970, he became the first Black player to start a game and score a touchdown for the Aggies. His first touchdown was on a seventy-nine-yard pass reception with thirteen seconds remaining in the game as A&M stunned LSU 20–18 in Baton Rouge. LSU would go on to win the 1970 SEC championship while A&M finished the year with a 2–9 record.[11,12,13] That same year, TCU signed its first Black football recruit, Linzy Cole. A year later, Danny Hardaway was the first Black player at Texas Tech.

Meanwhile, on December 6, 1969, top-ranked Texas and number-two ranked Arkansas—both with perfect 9–0 records—met in Fayetteville, Arkansas, for the Southwest Conference championship in a game attended by President Richard Nixon and dubbed the "Game of the Century." In a dramatic finish, Texas rallied from a 14–0 deficit to win by a score of 15–14. That game has since been chronicled in a television special and a full-length book. What is especially memorable about this game, played twenty-four years after Jackie Robinson signed with the Brooklyn Dodgers, is that every player on both teams was White. Texas went on to defeat Notre Dame 21–17 in the 1970 Cotton Bowl to win the national championship. The 1969 Texas team has the distinction of being the last all-White national championship team. Thus, when the decade of the 1970s began, many southern schools had a couple of Black players, but no one had more than a handful.

The decade of the 1960s had witnessed major changes in the relationship between races, not only in Texas but throughout the country. Major legislation had been passed, and race riots had occurred. Black athletes during the 1960s went from feeling gratitude at being able to compete with and against White athletes to a deep sense of anger at the injustices that remained. On June 4, 1967, several of the top athletes in the country met in Cleveland to discuss issues of racial disparity stemming from Muhammad Ali refusing to enter the military as a conscientious objector. Attendees at this meeting included Ali, Bill Russell, Jim Brown, and Lew Alcindor (later Kareem Abdul-Jabbar). This recognition of remaining injustices reached new heights at the 1968 Summer Olympics in Mexico City when Tommie Smith and John Carlos, who had won the gold and bronze medals in the 200-meter run for the United States, raised their clenched fists with Black arm bands during the award ceremony while the national anthem was being played. There was little question that more major changes were on their way. Further, it was during this time that more effective approaches in opposition to school integration emerged that were based on subtlety rather than direct opposition. Direct opposition was more easily labelled as racism and was more likely to be avoided. These tactics are discussed in the next chapter.

Chapter Six

Texas High School Football
Integration during the 1970s

Although Black and White students had been competing with and against each other on the football field for several years, a dual school system was still very much in existence when the decade of the 1970s began. In many communities, especially in the eastern part of the state, both the former Black school and the former White school were still in operation. Attendance was often determined by a freedom of choice plan designed to maintain de facto segregation. As a result, many small and medium-sized communities still had easily identifiable Black and White schools. For example, in Bryan in 1970, sixteen years after *Brown* ended legal segregation, both Kemp High (the former Black school) and Stephen F. Austin High (the former White school) remained in operation. Pictures of the high school football teams taken that fall show an all-Black Kemp High team and an all-White Stephen F. Austin team.

However, more change was on the way, much of it mandated by the courts. In 1968, the Supreme Court ruled on a case related to the freedom of choice plans that were in operation throughout the South. The specific case involved the freedom of choice plan of New Kent County, near Richmond, Virginia. In *Green v. County School Board of New Kent County*, the court ruled that freedom of choice plans are inadequate to meet desegregation requirements since the plans result in schools that remain essentially segregated and unequal. With this new policy in place, Texas school districts began to face greater pressure from the courts. In 1969, in *United States v. Tatum Independent School District*, the US Court for the Eastern District of Texas ordered Tatum and Mayflower schools to be merged. In the summer of 1970, eighteen other Texas school districts were taken to court for non-compliance with school desegregation measures. An additional forty-eight school districts were notified that they were being considered for court action. Consequently, methods to truly integrate the schools were implemented in many Texas communities. In Bryan, for example, both Kemp and Stephen F. Austin were converted into campuses for lower grades, and all high school students in the city, regardless of race, were admitted to the newly constructed Bryan High School. In the years to come, all four of my children graduated from a thoroughly integrated Bryan High School. Similar events occurred in city after city throughout the South. As a result, there is little question that during the 1970s, the most thoroughly integrated schools in the nation were in the small and medium-sized communities in the South where every student in the community attended the same school.[1]

School integration was not without its costs. Joe Washington Sr., head football coach at Port Arthur Lincoln, a former PVIL school, stated, "When integration came, I felt that they threw us a curve. They said, 'We're going to fix you, we're going to do away with your schools and bring your kids over to us.' They put those kids in situations that were new to them, and some of them were not able to handle it. Yes, we were probably better off educationally, but not as a race. We lost too many people in the shuffle. Coaches and teachers lost their jobs, and kids dropped out of school."[2] With integration, Black parents were sending their children to schools they did not know, and their children were taught by teachers and coaches they did not know. No question, important aspects of Black culture were lost.

In larger cities, the degree of integration was never as complete as in places like Bryan or Brownwood, because cities had multiple schools and school districts that had been extensively racially segregated by residential area due to redlining and simple economic differences across races over time. Although nobody recognized it at the time, the 1970s saw the high tide of racial integration of schools in the state of Texas and throughout the nation. It was during the 1970s that opposition approaches to school integration became more refined and began to have impacts. Another critical reason that integration progress stalled was changes in court and legislative policies. Instead of pushing for further integration, courts and the legislatures began eroding existing policies. In the end, school desegregation was no match for the clever adaptations of institutional racism.

The Supreme Court's change of direction was largely a result of the four conservative Supreme Court Justices appointed by Richard Nixon— Warren Burger, Harry Blackmun, Lewis Powell, and William Rehnquist. Two critically significant court decisions were issued by the new court early in the 1970s. In *San Antonio v. Rodriguez* (1973) the court ruled that San Antonio school financing, which was based on local property taxes, was not a violation of the Fourteenth Amendment's equal protection clause. In San Antonio and most other cities, school districts in wealthy areas had vastly more money per student than school districts in low-income areas, because the value of property in wealthy areas was much greater than in poor areas. The courts ruled that even though this approach to school financing meant widely different educational opportunities for children, this disparity was not a violation of the equal protection clause of the Fourteenth Amendment because education is not a fundamental right.

Also significant was the Supreme Court decision in *Milliken v. Bradley* (1974). This case involved plans to achieve school integration by busing students across school district boundaries throughout the fifty-three school districts comprising the Detroit, Michigan, metropolitan area. Detroit, like many other major metropolitan areas, consisted of a largely minority central city surrounded by mostly White and affluent suburbs. In the decision, the Supreme Court differentiated between "de jure" and "de facto" segregation and ruled that "de facto" segregation is allowed if it is not the explicit policy of the school district. This court decision ruled out the option of reducing segregation levels by busing students across district boundaries. This ruling effectively made full integration impossible in communities with multiple school districts with varying demographics. Foreseeing the long-term consequences of this decision, Justice Thurgood Marshall in his dissent stated:

> Because of the already high and rapidly increasing percentage of Negro students in the Detroit system, as well as the prospect of white flight, a Detroit-only plan simply has no hope of achieving actual desegregation. Under such a plan, white and Negro students will not go to school together. Instead, Negro children will continue to attend all-Negro schools.[3]

With this ruling in place, long-established de facto segregation would result in schools that were increasingly racially segregated. Speaking of de facto segregation, Black sociologist James Baldwin stated in 1965, "De facto segregation means Negroes are segregated, but nobody did it."[4]

After *Rodriguez* and *Milliken*, it was nearly impossible to do anything about the vastly unequal schools the existed from one community to another and in different parts of large metropolitan areas. *Rodriguez* meant that schools in wealthy communities had much more money per student than schools in low-income communities. This means these districts could build better facilities and hire better teachers and coaches. *Milliken* meant that it was not possible to bus students from low-income communities to schools in wealthy communities in which these students would have access to better facilities and teachers. As a result, the slow and relentless process of school resegregation began in the 1970s and continues until today.

The controversy over busing provides an example of changing circumstances and the more refined opposition to school desegregation that began to emerge in the 1970s.[5] Busing students to school had been going on for decades prior to integration. Busing made it possible for multigrade schools to replace one-room schoolhouses in rural areas throughout the country. Traditionally, most busing had been to move White children from their homes to schools. Rosa Parks remembered, "The whites rode buses, the Negro walked long weary miles in all kinds of weather."[6] The Reverend Theodore Hesburgh, president of the University of Notre Dame and a member of the Commission on Civil Rights, said, "I remember Medgar Evers saying that his first recollection of busing was the new school buses passing him and the other black children on the way to school, splashing them with mud as the white children on their way to a good school yelled out the window, 'Nigger! Nigger!' No objections to busing then."[7]

Opposition to busing became a politically effective means to fight school integration. A person could argue they were in favor of sending children to neighborhood schools rather than putting them on buses for more distant schools and not appear racist. Ronald Reagan used the opposition to busing argument effectively in his presidential campaigns, noting that busing had achieved neither integration nor better schooling. He also argued that integration efforts were based on the false notion that Black children cannot learn unless they are in the same setting as White children.[8] The consequence of these anti-busing and other efforts was that support for policies to increase integration levels began to falter.

Dallas and Houston provide vivid examples of the issues involved in school integration in major cities, especially after *Rodriguez* and *Milliken*. Dallas schools had claimed to be integrated for years. In 1970, Sam Tasby, a Black parent living in Dallas, sued the Dallas Independent School District, maintaining that his children were still attending inferior segregated schools. In *Tasby v. Estes*, the courts ruled that Dallas schools were, in fact, segregated, and steps needed to be taken to alter this situation.

As busing and other options were being weighed to more thoroughly integrate Dallas schools, a massive "white flight" occurred as White families fled the city for the suburbs. The results were astounding. In 1970, there were 94,383 White students attending DISD schools. A decade later in 1980, this number was down to 42,030. By 2008, there were only 7,207 White students attending DISD schools. The Oak Cliff neighborhood of South Dallas provides a vivid case-in-point. During the early decades of the twentieth century, most Oak Cliff residents were White and were served by segregated White high schools such as Carter, Kimball, and South Oak Cliff. Black students in the Oak Cliff area attended Roosevelt High. In 1966, the first Black students were admitted to South Oak Cliff High School. Within four years, the school had transitioned from an all-White school to an almost entirely all-Black school. With white flight following further integration in 1970, other Oak Cliff schools, such as Carter and Kimball, quickly made the transition from White to predominately Black schools. By the 2020s, some of the high schools in the Oak Cliff area, such as Molina and Sunset, were almost entirely Hispanic. Often white flight was encouraged by real estate agents who went door-to-door in some neighborhoods telling White families they needed to sell before property values crashed. The agents made significant profits because so many homes were changing hands. By 2021, only 4.7 percent of DISD students were White. The inner ring of Dallas suburbs, such as Garland and Irving, initially boomed during the 1970s as White families fled the city for the suburbs. These inner suburbs were then experiencing another round of white flight as families moved to more remote outer suburbs. For example, in the suburban Irving school district, only about 8 percent of students were white in 2021.

Highland Park provides an enlightening sidelight to the story of school integration in Dallas. The community of Highland Park is located just north of downtown Dallas. In 1913 Highland Park residents asked to be incorporated into the City of Dallas. They were refused and so incorporated their own city. Highland Park ISD was then created to provide schools for Highland Park children. As Dallas grew, Highland Park ISD was soon surrounded by Dallas and its school district. Dallas later made numerous attempts to annex Highland Park, but now their efforts were strongly resisted by Highland Park residents. Highland Park residents tended to be rather wealthy, and many had Black servants. The children of these Black servants were the only Black students living in Highland Park. Redlining and high housing costs prevented other Black families from moving into the community. Rather than develop a segregated school, the few Black students in Highland Park were sent to the segregated schools in Dallas ISD.

After the *Brown* decision, a city Alderman asked Highland Park residents to fire any Black servants with children so they wouldn't have to worry about school desegregation. Consequently, soon there were no Black students living in Highland Park and so the Highland Park ISD didn't have to integrate their schools. When Dallas schools began to experience extensive white flight in the 1970s as a result of school integration, Highland Park ISD was not affected. In fact, because many people desired to live near downtown Dallas, Highland Park provided an opportunity for people to reside near downtown and avoid a long commute, and they wouldn't have to worry about sending their children to integrated schools. With increased demand for housing, property values in Highland Park skyrocketed, and the community transitioned from a wealthy community to an extremely wealthy community. Highland Park schools continued to remain almost completely White during the ensuing decades, because there were few minority families who could afford the cost of Highland Park housing.

Circumstances were similar in Houston. By 1970, it was clear that additional steps would be taken to desegregate Houston schools. As in Dallas, the consequence was white flight from Houston ISD to the suburbs. By 2021, only 5 percent of HISD students were White. To provide a couple of examples, Sterling High transitioned from being a White high school to being a predominately Black high school, while most of the students at Milby High (a former White school) were then Hispanic. As in Dallas, the inner ring of suburban school districts (such as Aldine, Alief, and Pasadena) initially grew rapidly as people fled the city. In recent years, these districts have become predominately minority as White families have moved from them to more remote suburbs. The Houston metro area's growth has reached communities like Katy and Cypress, which were once considered distant outliers.

Spring Branch is a Houston example similar to Highland Park. Spring Branch ISD was created in the late 1800s in an unincorporated area outside of Houston. As Houston grew, the city annexed land as they expanded outward. Eventually, nearly all of the land in Spring Branch ISD was part of the City of Houston. The area, however, remained in Spring Branch ISD and was not a part of Houston ISD. The lone exception to annexation by the City of Houston was an enclave named Hedwig Village. Hedwig Village was successfully incorporated in December 1954, just a few months after the *Brown* decision. Memorial High School is a wealthy school located in Hedwig Village and part of Spring Branch ISD. The Spring Branch area now has an extensive population of minorities who attend other high schools in the district. Memorial High retains its exclusivity by requiring students to attend the school to which their residence is zoned. Thus, to attend Memorial High, it is necessary to live in Hedwig Village or select areas nearby. Housing costs are exorbitant in these areas, and thus Memorial High remains predominately White and wealthy.

Despite integration progress in some medium-sized cities during the 1970s, significant segregation remained in other Texas communities, and all-Black schools could be found that were not deep in the heart of big cities. For example, Beaumont Hebert, Beaumont Charlton-Pollard, and Port Arthur Lincoln remained in operation as virtually all-Black schools throughout the 1970s. In 1976, Beaumont Hebert made history by becoming the first all-Black former PVIL school to win a UIL state football championship. That year, Hebert rolled to a 15–0 record and crushed Gainesville 35–7 in the 3A state championship game.

The school integration that did occur in about 1970 often met signif-icant resistance. Longview is an East Texas city of about eighty thou-sand residents. Despite the city's relatively small size, it is served by four different school districts, which the community created and later maintained, in part, to facilitate first legal and later de facto segregation. The Longview Independent School District has long served the highest number of Black students in the city. After the *Brown* court decision, the city strongly resisted integration for as long as possible and continued to maintain separate schools for White and Black students. When total segregation was no longer possible, the school districts then practiced tokenism utilizing freedom of choice plans to maintain nearly complete de facto segregation. Then, in 1970, the courts ordered the Black schools in Longview ISD to be closed and all Black students to be bused to the White schools. On the evening of July 4, 1970, thirty-six Longview school buses were set on fire by explosives in an attempt to prevent busing and school integration from occurring. Two men were later arrested and given eleven-year prison sentences and $11,000 in fines for the bombings. Despite the bombings, integration proceeded. A month later, Black and White high school football players gathered for practice with their newly integrated football team.

In other places, the integration process was much smoother, and during the 1970s Black students were fully participating on thoroughly racially integrated teams throughout the state. Consequently, media coverage of Black athletes increased, and the facilities and equipment available to Black athletes improved. Among the most dominant teams during the 1970s included some thoroughly integrated high schools in medium-sized cities or socioeconomically diverse suburbs. For example, in Plano, a suburb north of Dallas, the Black high school was closed in 1964. The following year—the first year of integration—the school won its first state championship. Plano High won another state champion-ship in 1967. During the decade of the 1970s, Plano High had a record of 107–16–4 and won two more state championships in 1971 and 1977. In the city of Temple in Central Texas, the Black high school in the city (Dunbar) was closed in 1968, and Temple High School became fully integrated. After a few years of adjustment, the Temple Wildcats began a long string of successful football seasons. In the decade beginning in 1972, Temple won one hundred games, while losing only fifteen, with two ties. Temple lost the 1976 State Championship game, but then won it all in 1979.

Opportunities for Black athletes increased dramatically as college programs throughout the South began to open their doors to the best athletes available, including Black athletes. In a few years, southern college and university athletic programs had gone from complete segregation, to admitting a few token Black athletes, to wide open doors. Legendary Texas A&M University football coach R. C. Slocum described to me how this process occurred at Texas A&M.[9] Following a 5–6 record in 1971, A&M fired head coach Gene Stallings and replaced him with Emory Bellard, University of Texas offensive coordinator and inventor of the wishbone. During the Stallings era, A&M had admitted their first Black walk-on football players and had even recruited their first scholarship Black athlete, Jerry Honore from Lake Charles, Louisiana. The A&M recruitment of Black athletes at this time could be described as tokenism and was consistent with most other southern universities at the time; many schools had from two to four Black players, but no more.

In one of his first meetings with his new coaching staff, which included Slocum, Bellard was sending his assistant coaches on the road to recruit, pointing out the team desperately needed a talent upgrade. One assistant coach asked how many Black athletes they could recruit, assuming there would be a quota. Bellard's response was that he didn't care about race; he wanted good young men who were good football players. As a result, the 1972 recruiting class at Texas A&M had nine Black athletes, a dramatic increase from the tokenism of previous years. The policy of recruiting top Black athletes continued into future years, and in 1975 the thoroughly integrated Aggies were 10–0 and ranked number two in the nation before a season-ending loss to Arkansas dropped them into a three-way tie for the Southwest Conference championship with Texas and Arkansas. Other schools followed, and by the mid-1970s, top Black athletes were being recruited heavily by virtually every university in the country, including nearly all the major southern schools.

One of the Black athletes recruited by the Aggies in 1972 was Bubba Bean. Bean grew up in a small Black community named Call, just outside of the town of Kirbyville in East Texas. The Black kids in town attended the segregated Call School, which provided education for students from first through twelfth grades. Bean described to me how the neighborhood kids played football during his childhood.[10] They would start at one end of the field, and one of the kids would start running with the ball toward the "goal line" at the other end. All the other kids would try to tackle the ball carrier. Everyone was against the ball carrier. When the ball carrier was tackled, he would leave the ball on the ground where one of the other kids would pick up the ball and start running. Again, it was everyone against a different ball carrier. This process would continue until someone was able to cross the goal line.

Prior to Bean's seventh grade year in school, the Kirbyville school district announced that their schools were desegregated and implemented a "freedom of choice" plan. Bean elected to enroll in Kirbyville schools because the Call School didn't offer athletics. Bean enjoyed athletics because he felt discrimination was more difficult. In a track meet, if you ran faster than everyone else, they would have to give you the first-place prize. Bean was soon a star football player and was receiving recruiting calls from colleges around the country. R. C. Slocum was an assistant coach at Kansas State at the time and made a special effort to recruit Bean. Then one day, Coach Slocum came to visit Bean and said, "You know it gets awfully cold in the winter in Kansas. You should stay in Texas to play college ball." Slocum had just been hired as an assistant coach at Texas A&M by Emory Bellard. Bean went to A&M where he started for four years and was then a first-round draft choice of the NFL's Atlanta Falcons.

With more opportunities and more coverage, the number of Black high school football stars seemed to mushroom during the 1970s. A few of the many that could be mentioned are discussed below. A few years after fully integrating in 1968, tiny Big Sandy High School, located deep in the East Texas woods, set off on a five-year rampage, winning 62 games, losing only one, and tying one. During this time, they won three consecutive state championships. One year they scored 824 points (an average of nearly fifty-nine points per game), while giving up only sixteen points all year. They were led by Black running backs Bobby Mitchell and David Overstreet. Overstreet went on to play for Oklahoma and spent several years in the NFL.

Earl Campbell of John Tyler High School in Tyler led his school to the state championship in 1973 and then signed with the University of Texas. He was twice a first team all-American at Texas and won the 1977 Heisman Trophy. In 1978, the Houston Oilers selected Campbell with the first pick in the NFL draft. Campbell earned five pro bowl selections and a league MVP award in his Hall of Fame career with the Oilers. To provide an example of the benefits that integration provided for Black high school football players, Campbell insists that he was not the best athlete in his family. He stated, "If it hadn't been for the race problem, I would have been the third-best athlete in the family. Two of them were better than I, but they got caught up in the race thing and never got the chance."[11] Campbell was referring to his older brothers Willie and Herbert. They played football at the segregated Emmett Scott High School in Tyler and never had the same opportunities or visibility that came with playing in the UIL. Both went unnoticed while playing PVIL football and never got a chance to play in college. This problem was compounded because most southern schools were not recruiting Black athletes at that time. When younger brother Earl came along, Tyler schools were integrated. Earl received extensive coverage as he led John Tyler High School to a UIL state championship, and a scholarship to the University of Texas followed.

Not far from Tyler is the small town of Hooks where Billy Sims grew up. After a brilliant career at Hooks High, Sims went to college at the University of Oklahoma and was named all-American twice and won the 1978 Heisman Trophy. Sims had an outstanding pro career with the Detroit Lions before it was shortened by a knee injury. Another brilliant Black running back produced by Texas high schools during the 1970s was Eric Dickerson of Sealy. During his senior year in 1978, Dickerson led Sealy to fifteen consecutive wins and the 2A state championship. Dickerson chose to attend college at SMU where he teamed with Craig James to become the famed Pony Express. In his third season in the NFL, Dickerson broke the league record for the most rushing yards in a single season, a record that still stands. In his 2022 autobiography *Watch my Smoke*, he describes the racism he experienced playing high school football in Sealy and then throughout his college and professional career.[12] Joe Washington Jr. played for his father, Joe Washington Sr., at the all-Black and segregated Port Arthur Lincoln High School. He then played for Barry Switzer at the University of Oklahoma, where he was runner-up for the Heisman Trophy in both 1974 and 1975. He was the fourth player selected in the 1976 NFL draft and played in two Super Bowls with Washington.

Numerous other great Black players emerged from Texas high schools during the 1970s. A far from complete list would include lineman Wilson Whitley of Brenham, who became an all-American and won the Lombardi Award in 1976 while playing for the University of Houston. John Jefferson was a prolific receiver at Dallas Roosevelt and continued to excel at both Arizona State and in the NFL. Curtis Dickey was an outstanding runner at Bryan with the rare combination of exceptional size and speed. Dickey went on to become the all-time leading rusher at Texas A&M and was a first round NFL draft pick. Galveston Ball running back Charles Alexander went to LSU and established school rushing and scoring records for the Tigers. Kenny King of Clarendon starred for Oklahoma and later for the Oakland Raiders. Johnny "Lam" Jones of Lampasas became a star receiver at Texas and was a sprinter on the 1976 US Olympic team. Mike Singletary of Houston Worthing became an all-American at Baylor and an all-pro and NFL Hall of Famer with the Chicago Bears.

Given the chance to compete in integrated schools and an integrated UIL during the 1970s, many Black students proved they could excel not only on the football field but also in the classroom. As more and more Black and White students spent time together in school and school-related activities, stereotypes were crushed and a future with brighter opportunities for all seemed to be emerging.

Chapter Seven

Integration Flatlining during the 1980s

In many Texas schools, racial integration reached a peak in the 1970s. During the 1980s and 1990s, integration efforts stalled, and then the slow process of de facto resegregation began. This change of direction was largely a consequence of court decisions such as *Rodriguez* and *Milliken*, which were described in the previous chapter, and the lack of support for school integration by policymakers at the local, state, or federal levels. In Houston and Dallas, the consequences of *Rodriguez* and *Milliken* were growing rates of "white flight." In this new environment, White families could mostly avoid schools with large numbers of minority students by simply moving to a better funded, higher performing, and whiter suburban school district. White flight meant that schools in Dallas and Houston became increasingly populated by minority students. Surrounding the city schools were a ring of rapidly growing and largely White suburban schools.

In time, white flight reached the inner suburbs of Dallas and Houston as White families moved even further out. Thus, many of these inner suburbs were soon primarily populated by low-income minority families. White families who left the cities and then the inner suburbs were often replaced by Hispanic families The Hispanic share of the student-age population has increased dramatically in recent decades. In smaller and medium-sized communities, integration was more complete as all students in the community, regardless of race, would attend the same school. An increasingly important factor impacting school integration was the growth of private schools. In most private schools, a large proportion of the students are White. Private schools provided another way for families to educate their children while avoiding schools with large minority populations.

Texas High School Football in the 1980s

In this differentially integrated environment, two types of schools dominated Texas high school football during the 1980s. First were predominately Black, inner-city schools in Houston and Dallas that took advantage of the opportunity that integration provided for them to compete in the UIL against mostly White schools. The other dominant football programs in the 1980s were socioeconomically diverse schools in medium-sized cities with only one or two high schools or in integrated middle-class suburbs. In these schools, integration resulted in the dismantling of segregated schools, and all students in the city, regardless of race or social class attended the same school. In this chapter, powerful football programs in the city of Beaumont, Aldine, and Odessa Permian are described.

Predominately Black Inner-City Schools

Two predominately Black high schools in major cities were among the most dominant high school football teams in Texas during the decade of the 1980s. Jack Yates was established in 1926, then called Yates Colored High School, as the second segregated Black school in Houston. It was named for a prominent Black freedman and preacher who established Freedman's Town, now Houston's Fourth Ward, shortly after emancipation.

Yates competed in the PVIL until 1967. Upon transition to UIL competition, Yates quickly established itself as a state power and compiled a record of 113–16–1 in the 1980s. Prominent Yates players from this era included Dexter Manley, who went to Oklahoma State and then starred with the Washington Redskins (now Commanders) of the NFL; Albert Fontenot, who played college football at Baylor and then played in the NFL; John Roper, who went from Yates to Texas A&M and then to the NFL; and Santana Dotson, an all-American at Baylor and NFL defensive rookie of the year, who played in two Super Bowls with Green Bay. Luther Booker coached Yates High through the 1988 season. The 1985 Yates team is considered one of the best high school football teams to ever play in the state of Texas. The 1985 Yates Lions rolled through the season with a 16–0 record and beat West Texas powerhouse Odessa Permian in the 5A State Championship game 37–0. Led by running back Johnny Bailey,

Yates averaged 41.1 points per game, while its suffocating defense allowed only 4.8 points per game and had eight shutouts. The team was so deep that Santana Dotson, who was a junior at the time, had to come off the bench. There were eighteen Yates players on the 1985 team who earned college scholarships, and five players eventually played in the NFL.

If the 1985 Yates team was not the best high school football team in Texas history, perhaps it was the 1988 Dallas Carter team. The Oak Cliff neighborhood feeding Carter High had experienced white flight, and by the 1980s it had transformed from a White community to a community where nearly everyone was Black. In 1982, Dallas Carter hired Freddie James as head coach—and their football success skyrocketed. Carter won over one hundred games during the next ten years. During the early part of the decade, Carter had successful teams and produced numerous prominent players. The team, however, seemed to always fall short in the playoffs. Among the prominent players produced by Carter in the early and mid-1980s was Darren Lewis, who became an all-American running back at Texas A&M and is still the Aggies all-time leading rusher. Carter players Chet Brooks, a defensive back, and Rod Harris, a wide receiver, were Lewis's teammates at A&M. All three played professional football, and Brooks invented the nickname "Wrecking Crew" for the A&M defense.

There were twenty-eight players on the 1988 Carter High team that earned college scholarships and eight who played in the NFL. This included underclassmen who didn't get a lot of playing time during the 1988 season. The team was cocky and confident and rolled through the regular season undefeated. Then, the day before their first playoff game against Plano East, it was announced that a Carter defensive back/running back Gary Edwards had failed an algebra class but had continued to play—a violation of the state's "no pass/no play" policy. Carter was required to forfeit the games in which he had illegally participated, which disqualified Carter from the playoffs.

Edwards was initially given a failing grade by his algebra teacher. The Carter High principal then changed his grade to passing because, he said, the teacher had used a faulty and unauthorized grading procedure. An anonymous caller to the Dallas Independent School District tipped off officials that the grade had been manipulated by school officials to maintain Edwards's eligibility. District and state officials examined the grading book but couldn't follow the teacher's scoring logic. The superintendent of DISD ruled Edwards ineligible, resulting in Carter's disqualification, only to reverse his decision shortly after, reinstating the Cowboys in the playoffs. As Carter continued to advance in the playoffs, they were subsequently ruled ineligible again by the Texas education commissioner, only to be given an emergency reprieve by a district court judge ninety minutes before the start of the next round game, which otherwise would have involved their defeated opponent from the prior round.[1] Preparing for upcoming games was most challenging because the team was not allowed to practice during periods when it was declared ineligible. Finally, prior to the state semifinals, Carter was fully cleared. In that game, Carter defeated Odessa Permian 14–9, and then crushed Converse Judson 31–14 in the 5A state championship game. It appeared that for the first time since 1950, a school from Dallas ISD had won a state championship in football.

Unfortunately, the story doesn't end there. In a series of confusing events related to Edwards's eligibility, Carter was eventually stripped of the state championship. The championship trophy was then given to Converse Judson. The Reverend David Jones Sr., father of a Carter football player, expressed the feelings of many when he stated that White Dallas didn't want Carter High and Black Dallas doing so well and needed to find a way to put them back in their place. Many people in positions of power throughout the state were willing to believe that Carter was nothing but a Black football factory ready and willing to bend academic standards and rules to achieve success on the football field.

Carter's image as an outlaw program was compounded in the spring of 1989 when ten young men, six of them associated with the Carter football team, were arrested for a series of armed robberies. High School all-American defensive back Derric Evans, who had signed a letter of intent to play football for the University of Tennessee while sitting in a hot tub, was sentenced to twenty years in prison. Edwards, who had signed with the University of Houston, was sentenced to sixteen years. ESPN's 30 for 30 documentary series explored Carter's 1988 season in an episode titled "What Carter Lost."[2]

Even though some of the Carter stars went to prison instead of football glory, several other players continued their football success. Robert Hall had a fabulous career as quarterback at Texas Tech; Jessie Armstead

helped the University of Miami Hurricanes win two national championships and then helped the New York Giants win a Super Bowl. Armstead
was chosen to the pro-bowl five times and is in the Giants Ring of Honor.
Clifton Abraham became an all-American defensive back at Florida State
and played in the NFL; Le'Shai Maston was a running back at Baylor and
then played in the NFL.

In contrast to Yates High—which pulled students from a part of
town that had been the object of racist housing segregation policies for
decades—Carter pulled from the middle-class Oak Cliff neighborhood,
which had been on the other side of the proverbial railroad tracks. Houston's Third Ward, like Black neighborhoods throughout America, did
not receive investment from the city or local businesses, and its residents
didn't have the same access to jobs, transportation, or mortgages. As
court cases and legislation first began to end legal segregation, the Yates
community soon suffered from the loss of many of the area's wealthier
and more educated individuals who were able to move to better funded
schools and neighborhoods that had previously been off-limits. Those
left behind found themselves in worse conditions than before. In Dallas,
the Oak Cliff neighborhood was the destination for some of that city's
upwardly mobile middle-class Black families, and it remained a comfortable, middle-class community, but now inhabited by Black rather
than White families.

Carter football excelled during this period because it was such a high
priority to the community. People cared deeply about the games and a
variety of institutions were established to help young players develop
both their football skills and keep them off the streets, out of trouble,
and in school. Committed and talented adults living in the community
devoted their time and skills to assuring relevant institutions thrived.
Former Carter running back Greg Hill described to me what football
meant to boys growing up in Oak Cliff neighborhoods during the 1980s.
His insights likely apply to many kids everywhere.[3]

Hill was raised by his mother, a single parent, with help from his
grandparents who lived nearby. Hill's family struggled financially, and
his mother often worked two jobs to make ends meet. After graduating
from Carter in 1990, Hill signed with Texas A&M. Hill was redshirted
in 1990, then in his first game with the Aggies in 1991, he rushed for 212
yards in a 45–7 win over LSU, setting the NCAA record for most yards

in a collegiate debut. Hill finished his freshman year with 1,216 yards rushing, still a school record for freshmen. This earned him national attention and he garnered pre-season all-American designations before his sophomore year. Only then did his absent father make his first attempt to contact him.

The Aggies were in Anaheim, California, for a highly anticipated season opening tilt against Stanford in the 1992 Disneyland Pigskin Classic. The matchup of top-twenty squads drew the eyes of college football fans from around the country to watch the return of three-time Super Bowl champion Bill Walsh to the college ranks as coach of the Cardinal. Late the night before the game, Hill heard a knock on his hotel door from head coach R. C. Slocum. After a moment of panic, wondering if he or his roommate were in trouble with the coach, Hill let Slocum into the room. After dismissing his roommate so that they could speak privately, Slocum informed Hill that there was a man in the hotel lobby claiming to be his father and requesting to speak with him. Hill told Slocum, "I've got two fathers. My grandfather who helped raise me and you. Whoever that man is, he's not my dad." Slocum returned to the lobby and asked the man to leave. Greg Hill never agreed to speak with his dad until after he was selected in the first round of the 1994 NFL draft. When it became clear his father's interests were primarily financial, Hill ended the relationship.

As White residents fled Oak Cliff, many of the White-owned businesses and banks did the same. This left Oak Cliff and other majority-Black southern suburbs facing some of the same problems its residents had left behind when moving from the inner city. Many other kids in the neighborhoods feeding Carter High were in difficult economic circumstances like Greg Hill. For these kids, football provided a chance for success, respect, and escape, as well as a pathway to opportunities that others in the area had never experienced. Hill's idol while growing up was Darren Lewis who had played at Carter and then went on to become an all-American at Texas A&M. Hill saw how football had opened doors for Lewis and recognized that football could possibly do the same for him.

To be a member of the Carter High football team meant being recognized in the community. To be a star football player at Carter High was to be on top of the world for a teenage boy. While their fathers and grandfathers had played in relative obscurity in the segregated Prairie View League, the Carter Cowboys of the 1980s received extensive coverage from the *Dallas Morning News* and local TV stations. As Carter progressed through the playoffs, the team played in front of crowds of tens of thousands in major college and pro venues throughout the state, including Texas Stadium, home of the Dallas Cowboys. The fact that Carter could compete with and usually defeat the predominately White suburban schools was a source of great pride to the school, and the team received support from the Black community throughout all the Dallas/Fort Worth metroplex. The former Carter football players formed a proud and tight-knit fraternity. In the late eighties and early nineties, it was common to see a former Carter star playing on national television for a college powerhouse. They'd celebrate a sack, interception, or touchdown by finding the nearest sideline camera, pulling together a handful of his fellow Carter alums, and shouting, "Carter baby!" into the microphone. Despite the challenges of growing up in Oak Cliff in the 1980s, football gave kids dreams of a better life.

The neighborhood where Hill grew up had a strong youth football program, and from the age of eight when kids began playing, the games were serious, and the play was rugged. Even kids knew what was on the line. Those who weren't successful on the football field had to find other means of getting noticed and gaining respect. Unlike the middle-class kids living in the outer suburbs, many of these kids saw few examples of someone who had gone to college and developed a successful professional career; the easier path to attention, money, or glory was to sell drugs or be involved in other illegal activities. By the late 1980s, Carter High students would regularly see drug dealers and prostitutes and were faced with numerous other temptations daily. The fact that some kids succumbed to the temptations is not surprising.

Sports provided a pathway out of the inner-city for many other Black kids. Another example is Barbara Brown McCoy.[4] Barbara was raised by a single-parent mother who had six children. Barbara's family moved from inner-city South Dallas projects to Oak Cliff during the white flight era as Oak Cliff was transitioning from being a White community to a Black community. While in ninth grade, Barbara became a teen mother herself. This situation could of have ended her formal education, which then would likely have resulted in a life of limited opportunities, similar to what her mother had experienced. Instead, South Oak Cliff girls' basketball coach Gary Blair fought to allow her to become a member of the girls' basketball team. At that time, girls who were or had been pregnant were not allowed to play high school athletics. Blair's efforts were successful. Given the chance, Brown McCoy became a star player and led her team to the state championship. She was then offered a scholarship to play basketball at Stephen F. Austin State University (SFA) in East Texas. She then played on the 1979 US Pan American team and was a member of the 1980 US Olympic basketball team. The 1980 Olympic team didn't get to compete because of the US boycott of the Olympics in Moscow. Brown McCoy completed her degree at SFA and became a high school head coach and then the athletic director for Dallas ISD schools.

Also playing girls basketball at South Oak Cliff for Gary Blair during this era were Debra and Kim Rodman, younger sisters of Dennis Rodman. Dennis Rodman failed to make either the South Oak Cliff basketball or football teams while in high school. He was five foot eleven at his high school graduation, and the South Oak Cliff basketball team didn't have a place for someone that size who could neither shoot nor dribble well. After high school graduation, Rodman got a job as a night janitor at DFW International Airport. He then experienced a sudden eight-inch growth spurt, which prompted him to try basketball again. The rest is history. Rodman was on five NBA championship teams with the Detroit Pistons and Chicago Bulls and has been elected to the Basketball Hall of Fame. Gary Blair went on to a Hall of Fame coaching career, which included a national championship at Texas A&M in 2011.[5]

The rapidly changing racial demographics of Dallas and its suburbs produced another major controversy during the 1980s. In 1970, Norman Jett, who is White, became the head football coach at South Oak Cliff High. In 1970, South Oak Cliff was still a predominately White school. However, the white flight phenomenon had begun in the Oak Cliff area as Dallas schools were integrated, and the racial composition of South Oak Cliff, as with Carter and other area high schools, changed quickly. By the late 1970s, South Oak Cliff was a predominately Black school, and in 1987, 1,876 of the 1,895 students at South Oak Cliff—99 percent—were Black. Amid the rapid change around him, Jett remained as the football coach and was extremely successful at it. Over thirteen seasons, he compiled a record of 106 wins, thirty-one losses, and five ties. Jett achieved this success despite inadequate facilities. He constructed his own open air weight room, complete with truck wheels as weights and shingles to cover the dirt floor. His teams produced numerous college and pro stars. For example, after leaving South Oak Cliff, running back Wayne Morris played for SMU and then spent several years in the NFL. In 1981, all but two seniors on the team received college football scholarships.

In 1982, South Oak Cliff made it to the state playoffs and beat North Mesquite 36–13 in the first round before losing to Plano 14–0 in the second round. Following this season and despite his long record of success, Jett was fired as South Oak Cliff head football coach by Principal Frederick Todd, who had led the school since 1975. Todd then hired Edmond Peters, who was Black, as head coach. Jett later filed suit, claiming that his firing by Todd, who was Black, was a case of racial discrimination. A Dallas jury concurred and ordered the school district and the South Oak Cliff principal to pay damages. The case was appealed and eventually reached the Supreme Court in 1989. The Supreme Court ruled 5–4 that while Jett was a victim of racial discrimination, the school district did not have to pay damages because the discrimination was the isolated action of an individual and not the result of a "policy or custom" of discrimination. Even though Jett was White, his case was supported by the NAACP and similar groups. Civil rights groups viewed the court's decision as a major blow and another step toward school resegregation.

Economically Diverse Schools

The other dominant football programs in Texas during the 1980s were socioeconomically diverse schools. The schools in Beaumont provide a prime example. Theoretically, Beaumont schools had been integrated for years. When the 1980s began, however, there were two high schools in the city, located eight miles apart, that remained as segregated as ever despite the removal of formal legal enforcement of segregation. When the decade began, Hebert High remained an all-Black institution under the administration of the all-Black South Park Independent School District, while Forest Park was a nearly all-White school. Circumstances changed when US District Judge Robert Parker ordered that the two schools be merged in the fall of 1982.

When the judge's decision was announced, it brought howls of protest from both sides. The closure of Forest Park and Herbert was painful for many alumni, staff, and students at both high schools. Hebert, which was established in 1923 to serve the Black community, was a school rooted in Black history and tradition. While most in Beaumont's Black community desired integration, they feared the combination of the two schools would be more like an acquisition of Hebert by Forest Park rather than a merger of equals. As mentioned earlier, an integral part of the Hebert tradition was an extremely successful football program. Hebert High had been a dominating force during the PVIL days, and its success had not slowed down in the UIL. Hebert won a UIL state championship in 1976, and in its final seven years of existence the team won seventy-six games while losing only seven with two ties. In 1981, their final year of existence, the Hebert team won its first thirteen games and was ranked number one in the state before losing to Willowridge 15–14 in the state semifinals. Darrell Colbert was a junior on the 1981 Hebert team and told me the Willowridge game was the first time in his life he had ever lost a school-sponsored football game.[6] While playing in middle school and on the Hebert Junior Varsity, his teams had never been beaten. Colbert also told me that prior to his senior year, he had never attended school with even a single White student. Colbert and the other Hebert kids really wanted to stay where they were and graduate from Hebert.

In contrast, while Forest Park High had a long and eventful history, the Forest Park football team had not experienced the same level of success. In their final seven years they were 26–43–1. In 1981, Forest Park had gone 3–7 for their fifth losing season in seven years. Regardless, most students at Forest Park really wanted to stay where they were and graduate from Forest Park.

The result of the merger of the two schools was West Brook High, a new school with a new mascot (Bruins), new colors, new band, new cheerleaders, a new school song, and a new football team. Alexander Durley, a Black man who had succeeded Clifton Ozen at Hebert and continued their winning ways, was chosen as the head football coach at the new school. This decision brought protests from White people in the city. Durley had the almost impossible task of trying to make both the White and Black residents of the community happy, bridge the wide gulf between them, and somehow organize the collection of individual talent into a successful football team. School administrators told Coach Durley that they wanted equal numbers of White and Black players to start, which clearly limited the coaches' capacity to put the best possible team on the field. Durley refused to do it.

During the first West Brook football practice, Durley ordered the Hebert offense to scrimmage against the Forest Park defense. What followed was an hour of bone-jarring play that produced numerous bruises and near fights but also mutual respect. Durley then called the team together and said that never again would it be Hebert versus Forest Park. They were all a part of the same team now; they were all playing for the West Brook Bruins. Success would depend on everyone working together. Players told me that from that moment forward, while problems remained in the community, there were few problems between the White and Black players on the West Brook team.

Durley's West Brook team was loaded with talent. Its quarterback, Gerald Landry, would go to the University of Houston and become the Cougars' all-time total offense leader. Fullback Jerry Ball went to SMU, where he became an all-American defensive lineman and would later star in the NFL with the Detroit Lions. Wide receiver Darrell Colbert would play for Texas Southern and then for the Kansas City Chiefs in the NFL. Despite exceptional talent, West Brook got off to a dismal start. They lost their first two games to Port Arthur Lincoln (18–12) and Houston Kashmere (28–27). During early games, the Hebert fans would sit on one side of the field, while the Forest Park fans sat on the other. Emotions were high, and the community felt like a powder keg about ready to explode. In their final non-district game, West Brook finally got its first ever win, an unimpressive 14–13 decision over Galveston Ball. West Brook then lost two of their first five district games, giving the team an overall record of 4–4—a level of mediocrity totally unfamiliar to Hebert followers. The Bruins then won their final two games to earn a second-place district finish with a 6–4 record.

Prior to 1982, a second-place finish for a team would have meant its season was over. However, in 1982 the playoffs were expanded to the top two teams of each district. Thus, a 6–4 West Brook team barely squeezed into the playoffs. In its first playoff game, West Brook slipped past Houston Forest Brook 24–20. In its next game, West Brook tied Baytown Sterling 7–7 but advanced because it had more first downs, the tiebreaker at the time. In their third playoff game, the Bruins played Spring Branch Memorial, a wealthy, overwhelming White high school on the west side of Houston, led by future University of Texas quarter-back Shannon Kelley. Trailing 22–21, West Brook staged a dramatic ninety-three-yard scoring drive in the last minute to win the game. West Brook then began to roll. They outscored Dickinson 49–30, and in the semifinals beat Converse Judson 27–12. Judson had entered the game with a perfect 14–0 record and number one ranking. In the finals, West Brook earned the 5A state championship with a 21–10 victory over Hurst Bell. In the championship game, Darrell Colbert caught six passes for 118 yards, including a thirty-yard touchdown pass from Landry for the first score of the game.

When the Bruins finished the season with an 11–4–1 record, West Brook became the first school in Texas high school football history to win a state championship in its first year of existence. The Bruins were also the first second-place team ever to win a state championship and the first team to win a state championship with five blemishes on its record. More important than any of this was the effect the championship had on the community. The racial strife and tension that had plagued the school and the community were at least temporally forgotten as the football team progressed through the playoffs. As students and community residents watched the Black and White players work together side by side on the football field, they became united in their support for the team.

Racial tension in Beaumont remained just beneath the surface and would reappear a couple of years later as a result of more school consoli-dations and coaching changes. Prior to the 1984 school year, West Brook head football coach Alex Durley died suddenly of lung cancer at the age of forty-seven. He was replaced by Leo Nolan, another Black coach. Then in 1986, the three remaining Beaumont high schools were consolidated into two schools to complete the court-ordered integration. The students in predominately White South Park High were sent to West Brook, while historically Black Charlton-Pollard High and White French High were consolidated to become Central High. This consolidation resulted in the controversial shuffling of football coaches. At West Brook, Leo Nolan was reassigned, and former South Park coach Jerry Hentschel, who is White, was chosen as head football coach. Meanwhile, at the new Central High, Beaumont Charlton-Pollard coach Mike Mitchell, who is Black, was reassigned while former French coach Steve Shaver, who is White, was selected as head coach. Steve Shaver and French High had won a state championship in 1984. The fact that both Black coaches were reassigned leaving White head coaches at both schools resulted in an angry response from the Black community and an official protest from the NAACP. The situation was at least partially diffused in 1988 when Steve Shaver was reassigned, and Marvin Sedberry, a Black man, was hired as head coach at Central High. Thus, the de facto compromise was that the head coaching positions at the two high schools were to be evenly divided, with one Black head coach and one White head coach. These types of conflicts and delicate compromises in the partitioning of coaching jobs and other leadership positions in newly combined schools were common throughout the state.

Socioeconomically and racially diverse suburban high schools also experienced considerable success during this time. A prime example is Aldine High School. Aldine ISD is located just north of downtown Houston near the George Bush Intercontinental Airport. At the time of *Brown v. Board of Education*, Aldine High was a segregated White high school. As the population grew, other White high schools in the district were opened, all named for World War II generals—Eisenhower, MacArthur, and Nimitz. Aldine ISD also operated Carver High as the segregated Black school. As noted in chapter two, Aldine implemented a freedom of choice plan in 1964, which had virtually no impact on the distribution of students. That is, Carver High remained an all-Black school, while the White schools in the district each had only a few Black students. Like many other segregated Black schools in Texas, Carver left the PVIL and joined the UIL in 1967.

In 1975, Aldine High hired Bill Smith as its new head football coach. Smith had played college football at the University of Houston under Head Coach Bill Yeoman, who coached the Cougars from 1962 to 1986. Smith was at Houston when Yeoman recruited Warren McVey from San Antonio Brackenridge, becoming the first major university in Texas to recruit a Black player. While playing for Yeoman, Smith also learned the "veer" offense, which he implemented at Aldine High. For twenty-nine years, from 1975 to 2003, Smith coached the Aldine Mustangs and compiled an impressive record of 237–96–6.[7]

Shortly after Smith's arrival at Aldine High, Carver was closed as a high school following the 1977–78 school year as the result of a school board decision. Carver students were distributed to the White schools in the district. Two students impacted by the closure of Carver were Charles Benson and Robert Gipson. From elementary school through their junior year of high school, neither Benson nor Gipson had ever attended a school with even a single White student. After the closure of Carver, both spent their senior year at Aldine High, where they were members of the Mustang football team. At Aldine High, they joined forces with Coach Smith. In 1978, the talents of Benson, Gipson, and other Black players from Carver, along with returning White players, helped the more thoroughly integrated Aldine High win a district championship and earn a trip to the playoffs for the first time in twenty years. Gipson proudly told me stories of the integration process and the 1978 team. Gipson shared with me some old newspaper clippings showing how both he and Benson made the 1978 all-Greater Houston area all-star team.[8] Other members of this Houston all-star team were Eric Dickerson, Craig James, and Gary Kubiak. Both Benson and Gipson then played college football at Baylor, and Benson played for the Miami Dolphins in the NFL.

After integration, success continued for Smith and Aldine High. The school's greatest run of success came in the late 1980s and early 1990s. During this time the high school was about 50 percent White and about one-third Black. A number of Black students who attended Aldine High were bused from Acres Homes. Acres Homes was developed during World War I, and got its name because land was sold in acre lots. It was intended as a place where Black families moving to Houston from the country could bring their chickens, pigs, and horses. Because of a lack of services and opportunities, Acres Homes gradually dwindled into an extremely low-income Black community with the vices common to such communities in spades. Integration gave kids from Acres Homes the chance to attend school with middle-class White and minority students, and to play football for Bill Smith. Such experiences opened their eyes to the opportunities available in the larger world.

Pat Patterson, who was an assistant coach at Aldine High during this era, shared with me some stories of school integration during the early days.[9] One day he was driving his well-worn green pick-up truck to Acres Homes to meet with some of the Black players he was coaching. While at a stop sign, a young Black girl, maybe eight or nine years old was playing in the ditch near the stop sign. She glanced up at him and bluntly stated, "white trash." A week or so later, he was at the same stop sign, and the same girl was playing in the same ditch. She ran up to the door of his truck and said, "Coach, I'm so sorry about what I said last week. I didn't recognize who you were."

In both 1987 and 1988, the Aldine team earned a trip to the playoffs. Then in 1989, the Mustangs advanced to the state championship game played at Texas Stadium, home of the Dallas Cowboys, where they met undefeated Odessa Permian. This was the year after H. G. Bissinger had followed the Permian team and wrote his bestseller, *Friday Night Lights*.[10] The Permian team was led by several returning players from the 1988 team including running back Chris Comer and wide receiver Lloyd Hill. Quarterback Stoney Case would attend college at the University of New Mexico, and then go on to a six-year NFL career. The temperature during the 1989 state championship game was bitterly cold. Aldine lost four fumbles early and Permian jumped out to a 21–0 lead. The Aldine veer then started to chew up yardage. Late in the third and early in the fourth quarter, Aldine scored on a ninety-seven-yard drive that made the score 21–14. Aldine desperately needed a defensive stop to get the ball back to try to tie the game. Case, however, led Permian on a long scoring drive to seal a 28–14 win. Aldine rushed for 383 yards, while not completing a single pass. Permian was held to 268 yards of total offense. Aldine defensive lineman Steve Strahan told me that when the team came out to warm up prior to the game, they were freezing cold. They looked across at the Permian players who were in short sleeves, and he knew that they were going to lose.[11]

The loss to Permian was a major motivating factor as players prepared for the 1990 season. Numerous key players were returning, and much was expected of the 1990 team. Quarterback Eric Gray told me that he was especially motivated when he read a preseason magazine that said the team was loaded with talent but had a major question mark at quarterback.[12] The 1989 quarterback, Doug Womack, had graduated and accepted a scholarship to play football at Syracuse. In response, Gray worked extremely hard during the offseason. Each evening he would go for a long run with his mother following along on a bicycle encouraging him to go faster and further. As the 1990 season unfolded, the Mustangs crushed one opponent after another. They ran the veer offense to perfection. They seldom threw a pass and ran the same handful of plays over and over again. Players told me their opponents knew what play was coming, but still couldn't stop them. Offensive linemen Travis Coleman, Roderick Jordan, and Tremel Prudhomme told me how each of the linemen knew their assignments to perfection and the line worked very smoothly as a unit.[13,14,15] When teams overplayed the run, and Aldine did throw a pass, their speedy receivers like Eric Stevens could make opponents pay.[16]

The offensive players told me that while the offense was very good, the defense was truly outstanding. Led by defensive lineman Steve Strahan and Ervin Briley, linebackers Marcus Allen and John Lacy, and defensive back Larry Kissam, the Mustang defense stonewalled their opponents.[17,18,19] In most of the games, the starters played less than half of the game because the scores were so lopsided. Strahan later played for Baylor, Allen for TCU, and Briley for Texas A&M.

The Mustangs experienced a couple of difficult games during the 1990 season. The first was against a talented Kingwood team. Late in the fourth quarter, Kingwood led 21–17 and had forced Aldine into a desperation fourth down and eighteen. Eric Gray then hit speedy wide receiver Will Skinner on a crossing route, and Skinner raced untouched to the end zone for the winning touchdown. This Kingwood team later advanced to the state semifinals. After a relatively easy playoff win, Aldine earned a hard-fought 30–26 victory over Booker T. Washington, located in Houston's Fourth Ward, led by future University of Michigan star Mercury Hayes in the next round. For Aldine players from Acres Homes, the game against Washington held special significance. In years past, all Acres Homes residents had attended high school at Booker T. Washington, which was once a segregated Black school playing in the PVIL. Thus, most of the players' parents and grandparents had gone to Booker T. Washington. Later, boundary changes associated with integration had put part of Acres Homes in the Aldine district. Still the Aldine players knew many of the Washington players who were from Acres Homes, just on the other side of the dividing line.

In the semifinals, Aldine defeated Mission High from the Rio Grande Valley and quarterback Koy Dettmer 54–21. Dettmer is the younger brother of Heisman Trophy-winning quarterback Ty Dettmer. During the 1990 season, Koy Dettmer set a Texas high school state record for passing yards. This was the first time Aldine had played against a predominately Hispanic team from South Texas, and Steve Strahan told me that what he remembers most about the game is the Mission offensive linemen talking in Spanish to each other. The score could have been worse, but the Aldine starters played sparingly in the second half. Dettmer struggled against a fierce Aldine pass rush that sacked him numerous times. Larry Kissam intercepted three Dettmer passes, returning one for a touchdown. Dettmer went on to play college football at Colorado and had an eight-year NFL career with the Philadelphia Eagles.

In the state finals Aldine played Arlington Lamar, a powerful and unbeaten team from the suburbs of Dallas. On the morning of the championship game, Eric Gray learned that his cousin, who was a close friend and his same age, had been killed in a gang shootout. Gray told me that without football keeping him off the street, he could have been on the same path as his cousin. Gray dedicated the championship game to the memory of his cousin. He then rushed for 236 yards on twenty-three carries to lead Aldine to a 27–10 win and the state championship. The team was so dominant that ESPN named them the mythical national champions. The entire Aldine community was invited to an event where ESPN officials came to Houston and presented the team with a national championship trophy.

The Aldine players from that magical season have remained close as the years have passed. Many former players benefitted from attending an integrated school with solid academic credentials. As the demographics of Aldine later changed, they had jobs that paid well enough that they could afford to move out to suburbs that were safer with better schools. Several former Aldine players proudly told me about their children graduating from top colleges and then obtaining really good jobs. The discipline and hard work learned on the football field helped many players go from growing up in the projects to solid middle-class lives. Some Aldine players completed college with the aid of football scholarships and are now very financially comfortable.

Odessa Permian was another integrated and economically diverse high school in a medium-sized city that was extremely successful during the 1980s. In 1980, high schools in Odessa remained effectively segregated.

Minority students in the city were mostly served by Ector High School, which was 99 percent Black or Hispanic, with a total of nine White students. Ector was located on the south side of the city, where nearly the entire Black population of the city resided along with a large number of Hispanics. Deed restrictions had long prevented Whites on the north side of the city from selling homes to Blacks or Hispanics, and city ordinances blocked minority residents from receiving mortgages in redlined White areas. Permian, therefore, had nine Black students in a student body of 2,031. In 1982, US District Judge Fred Shannon ruled that the school district had effectively failed to comply with desegregation orders. While southside residents were thrilled with the order, they were angered by the solution. The school district closed Ector and bused its students from the southside to Odessa High and Permian High. Blacks comprised only 5 percent of the population of Odessa, and the 1988 Permian team had six Black players on a fifty-five-man team.[20]

The tradition of Permian football and the famed "MoJo mystique" was built throughout the 1970s, and Permian achieved an even greater level of dominance during the 1980s. During the decade, Permian won 122 games, while losing only eleven with six ties. Permian won three state championships during the decade—1980, 1984, and 1989. The 1989 team was undefeated and beat Aldine in the state championship game in the bitter cold at Texas Stadium. Permian became the archetypical big time Texas high school football program. Their home field of Ratliff Stadium has a capacity of 19,302 fans and nearly always sells out. The team charters jets to fly across the state for matchups with other top schools. Bissinger's *Friday Night Lights* describes the 1988 football season at Permian. Later a movie based on the book was released, and this was followed by a TV series.

On December 17, 1988, Odessa Permian met Dallas Carter in the state semifinals at Memorial Stadium on the campus of the University of Texas in Austin before a crowd of more than forty thousand. Cold rain fell throughout the game, making for terrible conditions. Permian scored first but missed the extra point to take a 6–0 lead. Carter then scored to take a 7–6 lead at halftime. In the second half, Permian blocked a Carter punt and used the excellent field position for a field goal to regain the lead 9–7. Late in the game, Carter quarterback Robert Hall hit wide receiver David Jones for the game winning touchdown and a 14–9 Carter win.

It could be argued that the Carter-Permian game was the end of one era, and that a new era was about to begin. Each team served as an archetype: Permian as the champion of a midsized town where the social life of the community centered on the exploits of the high school football team, and Carter as the urban school that attracted support from the Black community throughout the city, galvanized by the court battles to restored Carter's eligibility. These supporters saw in high school football one chance for Black youth to compete on a level field, while the educational and economic arenas remained tilted against them. Both sides understood the game had a deeper significance. Bissinger describes the meeting between delegations from the schools held at the Midland airport to negotiate the game logistics. Permian suggested holding the game in their Ratliff Stadium, while Carter nominated the Cotton Bowl, deep in the heart of Black Dallas. Austin's Memorial Stadium was accepted as a compromise. Everything was carefully negotiated, from the allotment of tickets to the presence of a large police contingent—favored by Permian, opposed by Carter—to the racial composition of the referee crew—a minimum of two officials would be Black. The final question to be agreed was the color of the uniforms. "The Carter Cowboys had their sacred red," Bissinger wrote. "The Permian Panthers had their sacred black. But someone had to wear an away uniform, and in this case, Permian didn't mind at all giving up black. It wasn't a problem. They would just wear white instead."[21]

In the new era of Texas high school football that followed, the success of economically diverse schools such as Odessa Permian, Aldine, and the schools in Beaumont would soon decline. In 1989 and again in 1991, Permian would go 16–0 and win the state championship. In 1995, Permian lost the state championship game to Converse Judson. Since 1995, Permian has never come close to winning another state championship. In the last three decades, Beaumont teams have often failed to make the playoffs, and when they have made the playoffs, they seldom advance very far. An exception was in 2018 when Beaumont West Brook advanced to the state championship game before losing to Longview.

Bill Smith's Aldine teams continued to have success through the 1990s. In both 1991 and 1996, Aldine advanced to the state semifinals. Since then, their success has steadily diminished. Likewise, the success of predominately Black inner-city schools such as Carter and Yates have also declined. Changing circumstances would open the door for wealthy suburban schools, and in the new era these schools would be dominant. Football success following wealth and power is not a new thing in Texas. In his excellent book about Texas high school football dynasties, Rick Sherrod noted that through the UIL's early decades, football success followed oil money across West Texas.[22] Football success would now follow the money to the big city suburbs.

Chapter Eight

The Resegregation of Texas Schools

By the 1990s, many Americans were celebrating the progress that had been made in race relations. The 'Whites Only' signs were gone, numerous Black people had been elected to high public office, and many Black athletes, musicians, actors, and other professionals were recognized as among the best in their fields. In Texas and around the nation, even the most elite schools had some minority students in their classrooms. There were no longer protests attempting to prevent minority students from entering schools. Much of the general public was convinced that the problem of school segregation had been addressed. For most Americans, the circle of acceptable classmates, colleagues, or even friends had been expanded to include minority people. At least those who were talented, educated, or wealthy.

But what about the vast numbers of minority people who do not fit comfortably in middle-class settings? In these cases, more subtle tools of institutional racism have emerged to keep the races apart. The effectiveness of these more subtle tools became increasingly apparent in the 1990s. In her book *The New Jim Crow*, Michelle Alexander stated, "We have not ended racial caste in America; we have merely redesigned it." She describes how Black and brown people were much more likely than White people to be locked up in prison.[1] Journalist Wesley Lowery provided evidence that Black people were also more likely to be the victims of police brutality.[2] Perhaps even more significant in keeping the races apart and slowing the social and economic progress of Black Americans were new policies that effectively resegregated America's schools. The visible impacts of school resegregation became increasingly evident during the 1990s.

The resegregated school system that gradually emerged beginning in the 1970s, and was increasingly evident by the 1990s, is very different from the segregated system that existed prior to *Brown*. During the pre-*Brown* era, the single factor determining which school a person attended was race. The modern system emerged gradually and is much more subtle; its outcomes are more complex. This chapter explores several factors contributed to school resegregation.

1. Legal Changes

Over several decades following *Brown v. Board of Education*, legislatures and the courts placed unrelenting pressure on communities to achieve racial balance in their schools. Although progress was slow, by the early 1970s schools everywhere were much more integrated than they had been two decades earlier. Then in the 1970s, desegregation efforts by legislatures and the courts began to wane. Public support for additional policies to achieve racial balance also largely vanished. The lack of public support for school integration is apparent from the strong public opposition to busing.[3] As noted earlier, the conservative court seated after the election of Richard Nixon implemented two major decisions, *Rodriguez* and *Milliken*, that greatly reduced the range of choices available to schools to increase integration levels.[4]

Several Supreme Court decisions since *Rodriguez* and *Milliken* have further eroded the foundation on which school integration had been built.[5] In *Oklahoma City Board of Education v. Dowell* (1991), schools were allowed to return to segregated neighborhood schools if the neighborhood where the school was located was already residentially segregated. In *Parents Involved in Community Schools v. Seattle School District No. 1* (2007) the court ruled that it was unconstitutional to use race as a factor in assigning students to schools. The consequence of the new legal environment is that families can easily avoid schools with large minority populations simply by choosing to live in predominately White neighborhoods.[6]

The end of redlining and other discriminatory housing policies also had a massive impact on predominantly Black schools and neighborhoods. At one time, discriminatory housing policies had forced Black families of all social classes to live in select segregated neighborhoods and communities. The end of these policies resulted in many middle-class Black families leaving segregated neighborhoods and moving to suburbs with higher property values, more economic opportunity, and better funded schools. These departing families had often been the leaders of the communities they were leaving behind. The decisions of these middle-class people to leave segregated communities were choices made independently by thousands of families simply seeking to improve opportunities for themselves and their children. Some of these families moved to predominately White suburbs, while others moved to middle-class suburbs where most residents were minorities. Left behind were the millions of minority people who couldn't afford to live in either the advantaged predominately White suburbs or the middle-class minority suburbs. These persons were left to live in communities where nearly everyone was a minority, nearly everyone was poor, and traditional community leaders were gone. Institutions suffered as a result. The schools in these communities are, in many ways, worse than the segregated schools prior to integration.

2. Demographic Changes

Demographic changes have resulted in minority populations increasing rapidly throughout the country and especially in Texas. These demographic changes have added another layer of complexity to school integration efforts. The Hispanic population has been growing especially fast. In 2022, for example, Texas was one of five states where a majority of the population was minority. (The other four are Hawaii, California, Nevada, and New Mexico.) The US Census Bureau projects that the country as a whole will become majority minority in 2043. In Texas, the Hispanic population alone now outnumbers the White population. These demographic changes have been even more dramatic in the student-age population. In Texas public schools in 2022, 51.8 percent of K-12 students were Hispanic, 29.4 percent were White, 12.7 percent were Black, and the remainder were Asian or some other race. In major cities with high levels of residential segregation by race, the overwhelming numbers and concentration of Black and Latino students in select neighborhoods have made it increasingly difficult to achieve any semblance of racial balance in schools.

3. Economic Changes

The United States has transitioned from being a largely middle-class nation to a country with a vast economic divide between the advantaged and disadvantaged. A critical factor in this economic divide is the growing importance of education. In the current US economy, persons without a college education are increasingly being left behind economically relative to those with a college degree. The gap between the incomes of persons with a college degree and those without is large and has become larger virtually every year since the 1970s.[7]

With so much of a person's economic future based on their education, many parents are deeply committed to ensuring that their children attend high quality schools that will increase their likelihood of being admitted to top colleges and getting a good job once they have completed college. The more abstract ideal of having an integrated school system for everyone has taken a back seat to assuring a quality education for one's own children. As a result, more completely rational decisions made by millions of families have led to an increasingly unequal school system. Economically advantaged families—doing what may be best for their own families—are moving to advantaged communities with high quality schools. By doing so these families are providing additional resources to help these good schools become even better. Meanwhile, poor families are forced into low-income communities with lower quality schools since they can't afford to live in communities with highly rated schools. Additionally, because schools are largely funded by local property taxes, schools in high-income communities have vastly more resources than schools in low-income communities. Modern highways and transportation systems have made it possible for people to live in ever more distant suburbs that have top schools and then commute to work, and an increasing number work from home.

Further, because of the strong overlap between race and economics, the system is relatively effective in keeping the races apart in schools. The system is especially effective in keeping kids from low-income minority homes out of advantaged schools. While most advantaged communities are predominately White, there are always some financially stable Asian, Black, or Latino families that can afford to reside there, giving the impression of an integrated school system.

The consequence of these trends is schools that are effectively seg-regated. Unlike during the pre-*Brown* era, schools cannot be simply dichotomized into White schools and Black schools. Rather, large high schools in Texas can be roughly categorized into four groups. First are the economically advantaged schools where a majority of the students are White, but with some minority students; second are middle-class schools where nearly all of the students are minority; third are schools where virtually everyone is both low-income and minority; finally, there are schools in smaller and medium-sized communities that remain integrated because every student in the community, whether White or minority, attends the same school. In chapter ten, examples of schools in each category are discussed with respect to their high school football teams.

Resegregation and Texas High School Football

Throughout this book, I have used high school football as a lens to ex-amine the consequences of school desegregation and the subsequent re-segregation. As schools resegregated, it resulted in noticeable changes in which high school football teams were dominant. In recent decades, the balance of power has swung away from inner-city minority schools and the economically diverse schools in medium-sized cities. Increasingly dominant are advantaged suburban schools and middle-class minority schools. Since 1990, no inner-city team has been as dominant as Carter and Yates were in the 1980s. Similarly, the success of socioeconomically diverse schools in medium-sized communities and middle-class suburbs such as Odessa Permian, Aldine, and the schools in Beaumont began to dwindle. Both types of schools were increasingly losing football games to wealthy suburban schools and middle-class minority suburban schools.

The reasons for these changes are rather simple. Several things are needed for a successful high school football program. Most obvious are talented football players and high-quality coaches capable of developing and utilizing available talent. Also important are family support and facilities. Top high school programs also tend to have quality middle-school and even youth football programs that increase interest in football and begin the process of developing future talent. In some communities, the same offensive and defensive systems are run from little leagues through middle school and into high school. As a result, when kids get to high school, they are running the same plays they have been practicing for years.

Wealthy suburban schools became increasingly successful by maximizing traditional approaches for developing winning football teams. Wealthy schools can afford the best coaches, and they have top facilities such as practice accommodations and weight rooms. These schools have strong middle school programs. The wealthy schools have strong family and community support. Further, wealthy schools can add components to the process of building winning football teams that schools lacking their financial resources are simply unable to duplicate. For example, many of the players on wealthy suburban teams attend off-season training programs, and many even have a private coach, all paid for by their families.

It was during the 1990s that the transition of power to wealthy suburban schools first became evident. Perhaps the first example of a wealthy suburban school with an exceptional football program was Austin Westlake. Westlake is a wealthy, predominately White, suburban high school on the west side of Austin. During the decade of the 1990s, Westlake won 126 games and appeared in the state championship game three times, winning it all in 1996. The 1996 Austin Westlake team, led by quarterback Drew Brees, finished the year with a perfect 16–0 record. Brees went on to play quarterback at Purdue before setting the NFL career record for passing yards and completions (since surpassed by Tom Brady). In his pro career, Brees passed for over eighty thousand yards, threw 571 touchdown passes, won a Super Bowl MVP, and will be a first ballot Hall of Famer. Westlake's success has continued into the twenty-first century. The blueprint utilized by Westlake to win football games was implemented by other wealthy schools as described in chapter ten.

Chapter Nine

Empirical Consequences of Resegregation

In this chapter, I examine data on Texas high schools during the 2022–23 school year. My goal is to present evidence of the vastly unequal schools in Texas and explore some of the outcomes of this inequality with respect to academics and high school football. In Figure 1, a comparison is made between the percentage of students in each school receiving free and reduced lunch—a measure of the economic circumstances of the students' families—and the academic rating of the school. All of the 5A and 6A schools in Texas in 2011 are included in the graph. Academic rating is determined by the percentile score on standardized tests averaged for all of the students in each school. This graph shows that the twenty-one high schools where 10 percent or fewer of the students received free or reduced lunch scored in the eighty-fifth percentile on average on standardized test scores. As the economic standing of families attending the school declines, academic test scores also decline. The forty-seven high schools where 90 percent or more of students receive free or reduced lunch on average scored at the eighteenth percentile on standardized academic test scores. The strength of this relationship is striking, and the benefits of having your children attend school with children from advantaged families is apparent. Among schools where 10 percent or fewer of the student body receive free and reduced lunch are Southlake Carroll, Highland Park, and Austin Westlake. At the other extreme, schools where 90 percent or more of the students are receiving free or reduced lunch include Aldine, Fort Worth Wyatt, and Dallas Kimball.

With respect to the racial integration of schools, high income communities with high quality schools where students score well academically tend to have a much larger share of White and Asian students, while Black and Latino students are concentrated in schools in lower income

Figure 1. Percentile academic rating of schools by percentage of students with free and reduced lunch

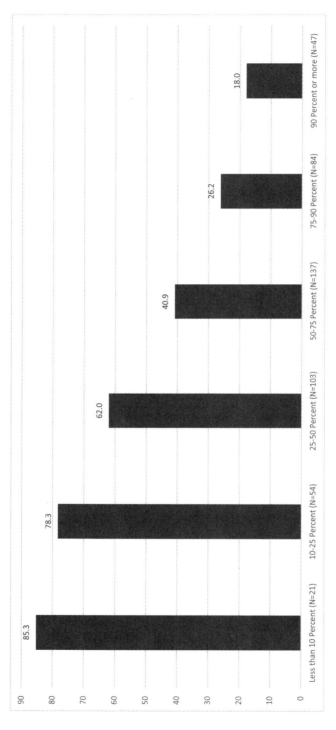

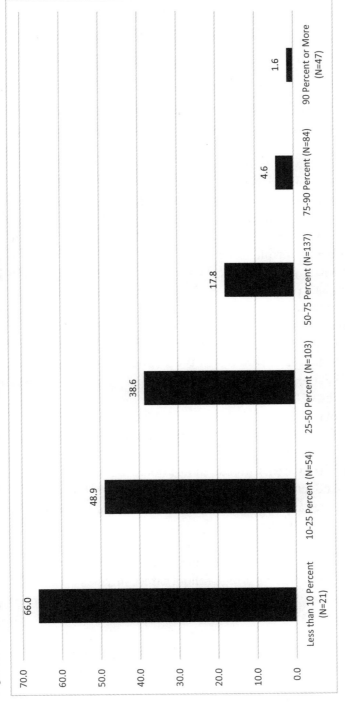

Figure 2. Percentage of White students compared with percentage of students with free and reduced lunch.

areas where the schools are generally lower quality. This is apparent in Figure 2 which compares the percent of students who are White with the percent of students receiving free or reduced lunch. While 66 percent of students are White in schools where 10 percent or fewer of the students receive free or reduced lunch, this percentage drops to 4.6 percent in schools where 75–90 percent of students receive free or reduced lunch and only 1.6 percent White in schools where 90 percent or more of students receive free or reduced lunch. Thus, while the advantaged schools are predominately White, they do have a substantial number of wealthy or at least middle-class minority students. Often, a high proportion of the minority students are Asian. In contrast, there are very few White students in the most economically disadvantaged schools. Thus, in Southlake Carroll, 61.1 percent of the students are White, 25.3 percent are Asian, and 13.6 percent are either Black or Hispanic; in Highland Park, 82.5 percent of the students are White, 10.5 percent are Asian, and 7 percent are Black or Hispanic; and at Austin Westlake, 67.6 percent of the students are White, 18.1 percent are Asian, and 14.3 percent are Black or Hispanic. In contrast, the percentage of White students is 1.7 at Aldine, 3.2 at Fort Worth Wyatt, and 1.9 at Dallas Kimball.

The consequence of this asymmetrical pattern of resegregation is that by the 2020s, the typical Black or Latino student in Texas attended a school with a lower percentage of White students than his or her counterpart fifty years earlier. More than one million Black and Latino students in Texas attend schools with few or no White peers. Furthermore, more minority students attend schools where higher proportions of their fellow students come from poor families. These schools tend to have fewer resources and lower levels of student achievement. Extensive research has found that low-income minority students who attend schools with more White students and more students from non-poor families receive extensive benefits ranging from higher test scores to higher graduation rates and better post-high school career success.[1]

As an example, Alana Semuals wrote an article in *The Atlantic* that describes a program in Massachusetts—The Metropolitan Council for Educational Opportunity, or METCO—that buses kids from inner-city Boston to attend school in the wealthy, largely White suburbs outside the central city. The results are impressive—98 percent of METCO kids graduated from high school, compared to 60–70 percent who were not in the program and remained in Boston schools. Further, 90 percent of METCO kids planned to attend college compared to 59 percent of students who remained in Boston. One program participant stated, "I was exposed to a lifestyle that altered my perspective of how things should be."[2]

High school football in Texas remains an illuminating lens for viewing society, and the trends of growing minority populations, asymmetrical resegregation, income inequality, and suburbanization have had a major impact on the sport. While Black football players are overrepresented at the highest professional and collegiate levels of the sport, Texas high school football has become increasingly dominated by wealthy and disproportionately White schools from high income communities. Figure 3 compares 5A and 6A Texas high schools on the total number of wins their football team had between 2011 and 2021 and the percentage of students receiving free and reduced lunch. To assure that the number of wins is comparable across schools, only schools that were in operation prior to 2011 are included. The most advantaged schools—where 10 percent or fewer of students were on free and reduced lunch—averaged 95.4 wins during this eleven-year period. It should be remembered that these schools are predominately White. As a school's economic circumstances declined, the number of football wins also declined. The economically poorest schools in the state—where 90 percent or more of students are on free and reduced lunch—averaged only 40.7 wins in eleven years. This gap in wins actually understates the chasm between football programs from high- and low-income schools as many of the economically poorest schools are in the same UIL district and thus many of their wins are against other schools with similarly limited resources.

Not only are the wealthier schools winning more football games, but they are also winning more championships. In Texas, both 5A and 6A are currently divided into a Division I and a Division II based on school enrollment. This means that among the state's large schools there are four state champions each year—5A Division I, 5A Division II, 6A Division I, and 6A Division II. In the twelve years beginning in 2010, there were forty-eight state championship trophies given out to the schools in the largest enrollment classifications. Of the nearly five hundred large high schools in the state, there are only twenty-nine schools where 10 percent or less of the students receive free or reduced lunch. Some of these schools are new and just recently opened their doors. It should be remembered

Figure 3. Number of wins from 2011–21 by percent of students with free and reduced lunch.

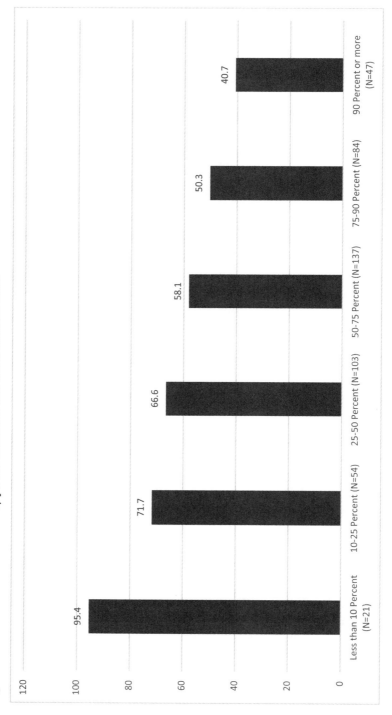

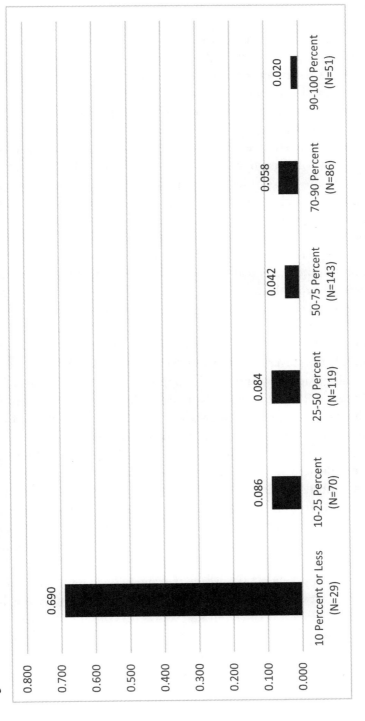

Figure 4. Number of 5A and 6A state championships per team from 2010–21 by percent of students with free and reduced lunch.

that schools in this category are predominately White. These wealthy schools won twenty state championships. Again, as the proportion of students receiving free and reduced lunch increases, the rate of state championships tends to decline, as depicted in Figure 4. Of the fifty-one high schools where 90 percent or more of the students received free or reduced lunch, there was only one state championship. This championship is obviously an exception to the rule and will be discussed later.

The wealthier schools that are winning football games and championships are also producing a large share of the football players heavily recruited by college programs. This is despite the fact that Black students are both way overrepresented among heavily recruited high school football players and way underrepresented at high-income schools.

Only a small proportion of the population is born with the physical tools to potentially play college football. Few people are big enough or have the strength and athleticism to play on either the offensive or defensive lines. Few people have the speed and quickness to be a wide receiver or defensive back. In addition to natural ability, there are numerous other factors involved in developing top-flight football players. These include the players' interest and desire, and the availability of coaching, training, facilities, and family support to develop the players' talents. Opportunities are enhanced among students from advantaged families who may have private trainers and coaches and the chance to play on elite teams where they are noticed by recruiters.

People with the rare physical potential to play college football could live anywhere. All else equal, one would expect top football players to be randomly distributed geographically. There are examples of great players emerging from every corner of Texas. However, some communities and schools are more likely than others to develop football players who are highly recruited. In some parts of Texas and the nation, football is a much more integral part of the culture than in other places. There are communities where kids dream of growing up to be football players; in other places kids dream of playing soccer or tennis or baseball. Some families are not involved in any sports. In communities where soccer is king, few football players are likely to be produced. Also, many kids who want to play football and may have the natural capacity often lack adequate coaching, facilities, or competition to develop their skills.

Figure 5 compares Texas high schools in terms of the percent of students receiving free or reduced lunch with the number of players from each school that were among the one hundred top recruits according to the website 247Sports. This website, which caters to fanatical college football fans who track their team's efforts to attract the next crop of stars, ranks the top high school football recruits each year. This analysis examined the eleven recruiting years from 2012 to 2022. Across Texas, there are over 1,800 high schools that play high school football, and many thousands of boys who participate in the sport each year. In a typical year, well over three hundred Texas high school football players sign national letters of intent to play college football, the official NCAA document that binds high school seniors to the college football program of their choice for at least a year. This is a very small proportion of Texas high school football players. Included among those who sign letters of intent are those who play junior college or small college football. Other recruits play for Division 1 or Football Bowl Subdivision schools that are outside of the most competitive conferences, namely the Southeastern Conference (SEC), Big 10, Big 12, and Atlantic Coast Conference. At the highest level, college football recruiting is dominated by the SEC and a handful of other top programs including Texas, Oklahoma, Ohio State, Michigan, and Clemson. These programs focus their recruiting attention in the state of Texas on the top one hundred ranked high school football players. The higher the player is ranked, the more intense the recruiting process. Many of these highly ranked recruits have gone on to great success in college and eventually played and become stars in the NFL. It should be noted that recruiting lists are certainly not perfect. Not all top one hundred—or even top ten—recruits have successful college or pro football careers. Others who don't make the top one hundred list go on to football glory. The likelihood of having a successful football career, however, is vastly greater for top-ranked recruits compared to those who don't make the top one hundred list.

In the recruiting classes from 2012 to 2022, just over half of the 5A and 6A high schools in the state had at least one person make the top one hundred list. However, wealthy schools produced significantly more top recruits than schools with few resources. Schools where 10 percent or fewer of the students are on free and reduced lunch had an average of

3.48 top one hundred recruits per school. Schools with between 10 and 50 percent of their students on free and reduced lunch had an average of about 2.2 top one hundred recruits, while schools with 90 percent or more of their students on free and reduced lunch had only 0.55 top one hundred recruits per school. Critically, it should be noted that 88 percent of the top one hundred recruits from 5A and 6A schools were Black, while only a small proportion of the students at these most advantaged schools are Black. Obviously, a significant number of the top recruits are Black students attending at least relatively advantaged schools where most of their fellow students are White.

It is safe to assume that the genetic capacity to play football is not limited to high-income communities; rather high school football players in these schools are successful because they have all of the structural advantages. These schools can afford the best coaches, they have the best weight rooms, and many of the players attend offseason camps or have a personal coach. Students with potential, but attending low-income schools are generally unnoticed and ignored, and their potential is generally never developed.

Of course, the benefits of attending a top high school extend far beyond the football field. I would also maintain wealthy schools that produce top football teams and talented football players also produce more students with the academic achievements that allow them to be admitted to the best colleges, often with scholarships that offset some of their college expenses. The end result is that these high-quality schools are producing more medical doctors, more lawyers, more business executives, and more engineers. In contrast, schools with large numbers of low-income students and poor football teams also tend to provide inadequate educational opportunities for their students, which subsequently limits future opportunities. It is tragic for the individuals involved, and tragic for our nation that so much potential remains undeveloped.

Figure 5. Number of top one hundred football recruits (2012–22) per school by percent of students with free and reduced lunch.

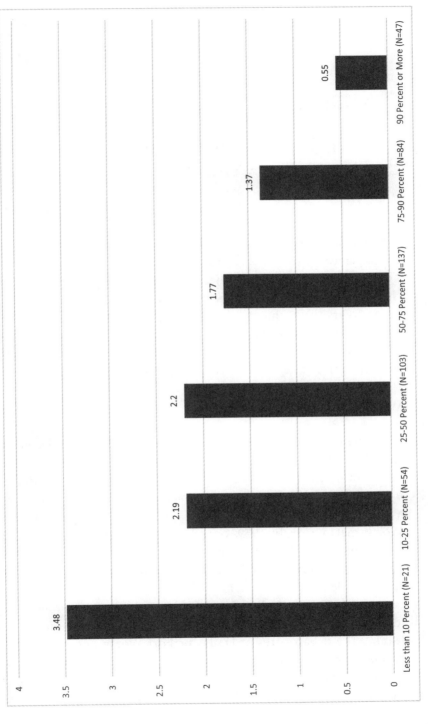

Chapter Ten

Texas High School Football in the Twenty-First Century

Throughout this book, I have used high school football as a lens to see the consequences of the desegregation and resegregation of Texas schools. Thus, as integration efforts stalled in Texas and elsewhere beginning in the 1970s and 1980s, the balance of power in high school football also began to gradually change, shifting away from inner-city schools and socioeconomically diverse schools toward schools in wealthy suburbs and middle-class minority suburbs. The implications of resegregation in each of these categories of schools are discussed below.

Wealthy Suburban Schools

With the decline of inner-city and inner-suburban schools, wealthy suburban schools have moved into positions of dominance. The archetypal example of a wealthy suburban school is Southlake Carroll. The town of Southlake was first incorporated in 1956 when it consisted of a few hundred residents living in the northern part of the Dallas-Fort Worth metro area. In 1959, Carroll school opened in Southlake for first through eighth grades, while high school students were bused to nearby Grapevine. By 1965, the school was expanded to include high school students.

In the 1970s, the Dallas-Fort Worth metro area was growing rapidly and expanding outward. With "white flight" many families were leaving the urban cores of Dallas or Fort Worth and relocating to spacious newly built homes in quiet suburban neighborhoods. The new suburbanites often commuted to their jobs downtown thanks to the newly built network of highways. By the 1980s, white flight was resulting in people moving to ever more remote suburbs, including Southlake. Not only did the Southlake population boom during the 1980s, the suburban community also became a coveted destination for many high-income families, most of whom were White. Million-dollar homes were sprouting up throughout the community. As the population and wealth in Southlake increased, so did the success of the Southlake Carroll High School football team. By 1988, the population of Southlake had expanded from a few hundred to over five thousand, and the school won its first 3A state football championship. This was followed by two more 3A state championships in 1992 and 1993.

In towns throughout the state—from Bryan to Temple, Odessa, and Longview—the high school football program had been a point of pride for generations. Especially following integration, high school football had served as a unifying force in the community. Southlake didn't have this history, but the Southlake Carroll Dragons helped convert the area from a collection of atomized neighborhoods into a community. Locals, including those with and without children at the high school, packed the stadium for home games, followed the team on the road, and were soon flocking to Texas Stadium by the thousands to watch the Dragons win more state championships.

During the 1990s, the Southlake population continued to grow, and the number of students at the high school increased. Soon the football team was competing in the more challenging larger classifications. In 2000, the school hired Todd Dodge, a former Port Arthur Jefferson High and University of Texas quarterback, as head football coach. Under Dodge, Southlake Carroll had a five-year run from 2002–06 during which the team had a record of 79–1 with four state championships. The team ran a sophisticated, no-huddle passing offense that was extremely potent and difficult to defend. High-level college football coaches came to watch the Dragons practice to learn from their playbook and practice sessions. The only blemish on their record was a 16–15 loss to Katy in the 2003 state championship game. During this run, Southlake Carroll once had a forty-nine-game winning streak.

Following the 2006 season Todd Dodge was offered the head coaching position at the University of North Texas, an almost unheard-of promotion for a high school coach. He left with a 98–11 record at Southlake Carroll. Despite Dodge's departure, the school's success continued. The

Dragons won another state championship in 2011. In 2018, Southlake Carroll hired its former quarterback and Todd Dodge's son, Riley Dodge, as head coach. Under Riley Dodge, the team lost the 2020 state championship game to Austin Westlake, which was then coached by Todd Dodge, who returned to the high school ranks in 2012 after his stint at UNT proved unsuccessful. In 2021, Southlake Carroll then advanced to the state semifinals and lost to Duncanville. Only twice between 2001 and 2021 did Southlake Carroll fail to win ten games. These were an 8–3 season in 2008 and a 9–3 season in 2015.

Success is not just limited to football. The school does well in other sports. Academic scores are exceptional. Average test scores at the school were in the 92nd percentile. The reason for such success is apparent. Nearly all of the students come from high-income homes (Porsches in the student parking lot are not uncommon), and less than 1 percent of students receive free or reduced lunch. School facilities, including the football weight room, are unparalleled, and the school can afford the best teachers and coaches. Most members of the high school football team attend training camps in the offseason, and many have a personal coach.

Southlake Carroll products include quarterbacks Chase Daniel, Greg McElroy, and Quinn Ewers. Daniel had a 31–1 record as starting quarterback at Southlake Carroll. His only loss was the 2003 state championship game against Katy. The following year, 2004, he led the team to a perfect record and the state championship. Daniel then attended college at the University of Missouri. In 2007 with Daniel as quarterback, Missouri was ranked number one in the nation and just missed a chance to play in the national championship game by losing to Oklahoma in the Big 12 championship game. Daniel finished fourth in the 2007 Heisman Trophy voting. After his college career, Daniel has been a quarterback in the NFL for well over a decade.

Greg McElroy moved to Southlake at age ten when his father, an executive with the Los Angeles Dodgers, was hired as the head of sales and marketing for the Dallas Cowboys. He led Southlake Carroll to the 2006 state championship and then led Alabama to the 2009 national championship. Following an NFL career, McElroy is now a football analyst for ESPN.

Ewers started at quarterback during both his sophomore and junior years at Southlake Carrol and was the preseason overall number one football prospect in the nation going into his senior season in 2021. Ewers, however, decided to skip his senior year in high school and signed with Ohio State. Before ever playing in a game for Ohio State, he then transferred to the University of Texas where he garnered national attention by taking advantage of newly liberalized NCAA rules regarding "name, image, and likeness," and signed endorsement deals with Aston Martin and Wranglers. In 2023 he led the Longhorns to the NCAA college football playoffs.

There were thirteen Southlake Carroll players that made the top one hundred recruits in the state between the 2012 and 2022. The majority of these players were White, but Black students were overrepresented relative to their 2 percent share of the student body. Ray Mickens was a Black cornerback from El Paso who starred at Texas A&M in the 1990s and then played eleven years in the NFL before becoming a successful businessman who owns and operates numerous restaurants. His NFL and business career provided the economic means that allowed him and his family to live in Southlake. His son, RJ Mickens, was a star at Southlake Carroll and then accepted a scholarship to play safety for the Clemson Tigers. Following a fourteen-year Major League Baseball career, Ken Hill, also Black, and his family moved to Southlake. Their son Kenny Hill quarterbacked Southlake Carroll to the 2011 state championship and then accepted a scholarship to play football at Texas A&M. In his first game as starter, he came to national attention by setting the school record with 511 passing yards. He later transferred and played quarterback at TCU.

As mentioned earlier, Highland Park High School is a wealthy, predominately White high school just north of downtown Dallas. In 1999, Randy Allen became head coach at Highland Park and a long period of success ensued. Through the 2022 season, Allen's record at Highland Park was a remarkable 282–34, and he'd won four state championships. Only twice have Allen-coached Highland Park teams failed to win ten games—in 2004 they won eight, and in 2012 they won nine. The first Highland Park state championship in the Randy Allen era was in 2005. This team was led by quarterback Matthew Stafford. Stafford's classmate at Highland Park was Clayton Kershaw, who would go on to a hall of fame career as a baseball pitcher with the Los Angeles Dodgers. Following his Highland Park career, Stafford was the number one quarterback recruit in the nation and chose to attend the University of Georgia. In 2009, he was the first overall pick in the NFL draft by the Detroit Lions. Later he was traded to the Los Angeles Rams, and he led the Rams to a win in Super Bowl LVI. More recently, Highland Park won three consecutive state championships in 2016, 2017, and 2018.

Aledo High School is a west Fort Worth suburb in Parker County. For decades, Parker County was culturally and demographically a West Texas frontier cowboy county. It was even home to Oliver Loving of Loving-Goodnight Cattle Trail fame, the inspiration for Larry McMurtry's *Lonesome Dove*. Similar to other West Texas towns, Aledo had a miniscule Black population of less than 2 percent. As the Dallas-Fort Worth metropolitan area continued to boom, Aledo became part of the metro area's outer suburban fringe. By the 1990s, Aledo was experiencing rapid growth. Especially significant was when Lockheed Martin built a facility on the west side of Fort Worth not far from Aledo. Lockheed Martin then built a golf course in Aledo, and many of their employees moved to the city. Most of the new Aledo residents were well-paid engineers and other skilled workers. Like the existing population, the new residents were overwhelmingly White.

In 1993, the school hired Tim Buchanan as its new football coach. In 1993, the Aledo Bearcats finished the season with a 2–8 record, but success soon followed, and Buchanan would never have another losing season. By the time of his retirement following another state championship in 2022, Buchanan had won 281 football games at Aledo High. This number would be greater, but there was a five-year period from 2014 through 2018 when Buchanan stepped down as head coach to be the athletic director, and Steve Wood took over as head coach. In 2019, Buchanan resumed the position as head coach. In the five years Wood was head coach, the team won three state championships. Coach Buchanan is one of only three Texas high school football coaches to win a state championship in four different decades. The other two are Gordon Wood and G. A. Moore Jr.

Beginning in 2009, Aledo High won ten state championships in a fourteen-year period. Since 2009, Aledo has won more high school football games than any other large high school in the state. Some of the Aledo High teams were truly dominant. In 2013, the Bearcats went 16–0 and outscored their opponents 1,023–147. The average score of their games that year 63.9–9.2. When I asked Coach Buchanan about his most memorable wins, he mentioned his first win in 1993 over Glen Rose, and two state championship game victories in seasons where the team was not expected to do well (1998 and 2022).[1]

Like other predominately White, wealthy schools (less than 10 percent of the students receive free or reduced lunch), Aledo has few minority students. From 2012 to 2022, Aledo had eleven players who were among the top one hundred recruits in the state; seven of the eleven were Black. Perhaps the best-known player from Aledo High is Johnathan Gray, a Black athlete and son of former Fort Worth Trimble Tech and Texas Tech All-America running back James Gray. Following an NFL career, James Gray and his family could afford to live in Aledo. While at Aledo High, Johnathan Gray became the second leading rusher in Texas high school history with 10,889 yards. He holds the national record for touchdowns scored (205) and led Aledo to state championships in 2009, 2010, and 2011. Gray was ranked as one of the top ten recruits in the country and signed with the University of Texas. He tore his right Achilles tendon in 2013 and his left Achilles tendon in 2015, which slowed his college career and largely ended his chances of playing professional football.

Another Dallas area school that has experienced significant success is Allen. Allen is an affluent, economically dynamic suburb north of Dallas. Allen High won its district championship and at least ten games every year between 2006 and 2021. During this time, Allen won five state championships—including three in a row in 2012, 2013, and 2014—under quarterback Kyler Murray. Murray is the son of former Texas A&M and NFL quarterback Kevin Murray. During the Kyler Murray era, the school had a string of fifty-seven consecutive wins. Murray was a top-five recruit and went on to win a Heisman Trophy at the University of Oklahoma, after which he was selected first overall in the 2019 NFL draft. In 2022 he signed a five-year, $230.5 million contract extension with the Arizona Cardinals. Between 2012 and 2022, twenty Allen players were among the top one hundred recruits in the state. Despite the fact that only 12 percent of the Allen student body is Black, nearly all of the school's highly recruited football players were Black.

Houston and Austin have also had their share of wealthy suburban schools with dominant football programs. Perhaps the most successful large high school football program in the entire state of Texas over the past couple of decades is Katy High School.[2] The Katy community got its name because it was once a stop on the Missouri-Kansas-Texas, or "K-T," railroad. Through the early decades of the twentieth century, the community was a sugar cane and rice growing settlement. Beginning in the 1960s and 1970s, Katy's population grew dramatically as the city of Houston expanded westward. Katy is now a relatively affluent and economically dynamic suburb along Interstate 10. While there are large numbers of White students at the school, Katy is more racially diverse than either Southlake, Highland Park, or Aledo, and is more similar to Allen High in the Dallas area. Katy Independent School District recently opened a magnificent high school football stadium that cost over $70 million to build.

Since 1997, Katy has played in thirteen state championship games, winning eight. During this run, only in 2001 did the school fail to win ten games; that year they won eight. Because of the school's long history of success, families with sons who are promising football players often move to Katy, where they get excellent coaching, benefit from top facilities, and play in big games that are more likely to be noticed by college recruiters. Between 2012 and 2022, seventeen Katy players were among the top one hundred recruits in the state, with significant numbers of both White and Black players. Among notable Katy graduates is quarterback Andy Dalton. Dalton attended TCU after his Katy career and has then had a long NFL career.

The success of Austin Westlake High in the 1990s has already been mentioned. Westlake's success continued into the twenty-first century with eight more state championship game appearances. Another prominent Westlake alum is Nick Foles, who graduated in 2007. After playing for the University of Arizona, he became MVP of Super Bowl LII for leading the Philadelphia Eagles to a Super Bowl championship. After hiring former Southlake Carroll coach Todd Dodge, Westlake won three consecutive state championships. Between 2019 and the state semifinals of 2022, Westlake had a string of fifty-four consecutive wins, with three consecutive state championships in 2019, 2020, and 2021. Their winning streak ended in the 6A Division I semifinals in 2022 with a 49–34 loss to Galena Park North Shore. Lake Travis is another wealthy Austin suburban high school. Lake Travis won five consecutive state championships from 2007 to 2011, and then won its sixth state championship in 2016. Well-known Lake Travis alums include Heisman Trophy-winning quarterback Baker Mayfield.

Middle-Class Minority Suburban Schools

In South Dallas, many Black families with increased financial means are moving further south from inner-city neighborhoods like Oak Cliff—where their kids would have attended schools like Carter, Kimball, and South Oak Cliff—to the suburban communities of Duncanville, DeSoto, and Cedar Hill. Driving through Duncanville, DeSoto, and Cedar Hill, one is struck by the fact that the communities seem so typically suburban. Setting back from tree-lined streets are neat, middle-class homes surrounded by well-kept lawns. These communities were once largely White suburbs. Duncanville High graduates include Texas Governor Greg Abbott and NBA basketball player Greg Ostertag, both of whom are White. A major difference between Duncanville now and Duncanville a few decades ago is that now almost everyone in the community is minority. In 1991, about three-fourths of the students at Duncanville High were White; by 2022, only 2.1 percent were White. Similarly, DeSoto High is now only 1.8 percent White, and Cedar Hill High is 2.9 percent White.

All three schools have experienced significant athletic success. Between 2017 and 2022, Duncanville has made it to the 6A state championship game four times, facing Galena Park North Shore each time. The first three times Duncanville lost to North Shore, before finally winning a state championship in 2022 with a hard fought 28–21 win. The Duncanville boys' basketball team won three consecutive state championships in 2019, 2021, and 2022 (with the 2020 tournament cancelled due to the Covid-19 pandemic). Later, the 2022 basketball championship was taken from Duncanville because one of its players, Anthony Black, illegally transferred to the school to play with more talented teammates, enjoy top coaches, and have a chance to win a state championship. Black was among the top basketball recruits in the country and chose to play college basketball at Arkansas. After one year in college, Black was the sixth overall pick in the first round of the NBA draft by the Orlando Magic. The Duncanville girls basketball team has won eleven state championships.

DeSoto won the 6A state football championship in 2016 and again in 2022. Cedar Hill won state championships in football in 2006, 2013, and 2014. These three schools now provide perhaps the most fertile recruiting hotbed in the state of Texas. Between 2012 and 2022, DeSoto had twenty-three top one hundred recruits—more than any other school in the state. Cedar Hill had sixteen and Duncanville fourteen. Graduates from these schools include Von Miller of DeSoto High. Miller played at Texas A&M, where he won the Butkus Award as the nation's best linebacker, and he was the second overall pick in the 2011 NFL draft. In the 2015 season, he was the MVP of the Super Bowl with the Denver Broncos. Later as a member of the Los Angeles Rams, he won a second Super Bowl ring. As of this writing, Miller has more career sacks than any other active player in the NFL.

Several schools in middle-class minority communities in the Houston area are also doing very well. A prime example is Galena Park North Shore. At one time, Galena Park was largely a White, middle-class suburb. Into the 1990s, more than 50 percent of the students at North Shore High School were White. As Houston grew and expanded outward, Galena Park became the destination for many minority residents who could afford to leave the city and live in the suburbs. There are now two high schools in the Galena Park Independent School District. At Galena Park High School, well over 90 percent of the students are Latino. North Shore High School is now 3.7 percent White, 23.8 percent Black, and over 70 percent Latino. North Shore High has won five football state championships, four of them since 2015. They also lost the 2022 championship game to Duncanville. From 2012 to 2022, North Shore produced fifteen players who were top one hundred recruits in the state, all of them Black.

Another school with high levels of football success is Manvel. Manvel is located in Brazoria County on the southern edge of the Houston metro area. Manvel is a part of the Alvin Independent School District. For more than one hundred years, Alvin High was the only high school in the district. At one time, Alvin was a "sundown" town where no Black people were allowed after sundown. Later, Alvin was the hometown of baseball Hall of Fame pitcher Nolan Ryan. Nathan Evoldi is another star Major League pitcher from Alvin. As the Houston metro area expanded into the Alvin area, many of the new residents were middle-class minority persons. As the population grew, a new high school, Manvel High, opened in 2006 and began playing varsity football in 2008. Manvel High has always had a much larger minority population than nearby Alvin High. In 2010, Manvel won its first district championship, and the next year, 2011, it made it to the state championship game where Manvel lost to Aledo. Beginning in 2013, Manvel lost in the state quarterfinals four straight years, including three times to Katy. Then in 2017, Manvel made it to the state championship game but lost to Highland Park. Between 2012 and 2022, Manvel produced nineteen top one hundred recruits, all but one of them Black.

I watched the 2017 state championship game between Highland Park and Manvel, and it was one of the best football games at any level I have ever seen. The game was made even more interesting because virtually every member of the Highland Park team was White, while virtually every member of the Manvel team was Black. Highland Park scored the game winning touchdown on a sixteen-yard touchdown pass from quarterback John Stephen Jones with thirty-four seconds left. The final score was 53–49. Jones, who is the grandson of Dallas Cowboys owner Jerry Jones, passed for 564 yards in the game. Like his grandfather, he then attended college at Arkansas. The two teams combined for 1,286 yards of total offense. Manvel wide receiver Jalen Preston, who later attended Texas A&M, scored on touchdown passes of sixty-nine, seven, and ninety-five yards.

With the continued rapid population growth in Brazoria County, a third high school in the Alvin school district, Shadow Creek, opened in 2016. In 2022, only 12 percent of the students at Shadow Creek were White, and almost half of the students are Black. Yet most students are economically comfortable. Academically, Shadow Creek is among the better schools in the state. Shadow Creek began playing varsity football for the first time in 2018. In their first year, they made it to the state championship game, where they lost to Highland Park. The following year, 2019, Shadow Creek went undefeated and won the state championship with a 28–22 win over Denton Ryan.

Low-Income, Inner-City, and Inner-Suburb Schools

In recent decades, inner-city and inner-suburb schools have never achieved the level of success they had in the 1980s. For example, Carter High football was dominant during the 1980s and produced some of the best high school teams the state has ever seen. Since 1991, Carter has never made it past the third round of the playoffs. Yates High followed a similar trajectory. Following their state championship in 1985, Yates made it to the championship game in 1992 and lost to Temple. In 1996, they lost in the state quarterfinals. Since then, Yates has never advanced deeply in the playoffs. The same is true of nearly all other inner-city schools.

There are several reasons for the decline of inner-city schools. Perhaps most important, a version of the white flight phenomenon in which White people were leaving the city seeking better schools in the suburbs also occurred with many inner-city minority families. Often minority families who could afford to leave the inner city for the suburbs did so when redlining laws were removed. Some moved to predominately White suburbs, others to middle-class minority suburbs. To some extent, those remaining in the inner city were those that lacked the resources to get out. The loss of capable middle- and working-class families had devastating impacts for inner-city schools, churches, and other institutions. A noticeable pattern emerged of institutions in low-income communities beginning to crumble. For the purposes of this book, a prime example is youth football. The success of institutions such as youth football requires the involvement of people with the time, resources, and management ability to make things work. Many of those who could have helped institutions succeed moved away and took their contributions to communities that already had advantages. Financially stressed people in low-income communities generally have neither the time nor ability to manage activities that improve the community.

The consequence is that since about 1990 most inner-city schools have become less competitive, and the team that wins the championship of an inner-city district is usually eliminated during the early rounds of the Texas high school football playoffs. Declining enrollment has meant that many of these schools have dropped to a lower classification. The loss of middle-class families means that in many ways, inner-city schools are worse off now than in they were prior to integration when capable people were helping their institutions run smoothly.

In September 2022, I attended a Kashmere High School football game. Kashmere is an inner-city Houston high school with a long and proud history. The federal Subsistence Homesteads Division built the Trinity Gardens subdivision, where Kashmere High is located, as part of the New Deal during the Great Depression of the 1930s. The purpose of the development was to provide poor and landless Black people with a chance to become homeowners. In their first year as a part of the UIL in 1967, Kashmere won a district championship. Kashmere has produced many players who starred in college and the NFL, such as Delvin Williams, Rodney Hampton, and Jacob Green. Williams played college football at Kansas and then played in the NFL. Hampton went from Kashmere to the University of Georgia. He then starred as a running back for the New York Giants and twice made the pro bowl. Green attended Texas A&M, where he became the school's all-time sack leader. He was then a first-round draft pick of the Seattle Seahawks where he played twelve seasons and is now recognized in the team's ring of honor. School success and achievement were not limited to athletics. The Kashmere Stage Band won national championships in the 1970s and was featured in the 2011 documentary *Thunder Soul*.

By 2022, the successes achieved in years past at Kashmere High seemed like a distant dream. At the game I attended, the stands were mostly empty, with total attendance of around two hundred people. Only twenty-three players were in uniform for Kashmere. The play was generally ragged. The Kashmere High football team has won only eighteen games combined in the past seven years. There were only four cheerleaders, and the band consisted of only six members, including three drummers. The band didn't perform at halftime. After watching *Thunder Soul*, I found the lack of interest in band surprising and disturbing. While at the game, I spoke with a former player who had graduated from Kashmere in 1983. He said the decline of the school makes him very sad. He remembers when he played, the stands were filled, the band was playing, and the place was rocking. He was very proud of the high-quality football that was being played and noted that many players from Kashmere and nearby schools would go on to play in college and the pros. Jacob Green told me that there were nine hundred students in his graduating class; in 2022 there were only 830 students in the entire school. He noted that many people he knew while growing up have left the inner city for the suburbs as they seek better opportunities for themselves and their families.[3]

Like inner-city Houston, the inner ring of Houston suburbs have seen their football success diminish. Aldine High continued to have successful teams through the 1990s and until coach Bill Smith retired following the 2003 season. They have had limited success since. Some inner suburbs, like Aldine, have also experienced significant demographic changes since the 1990s as both White and minority middle-class families have left the area and moved to more distant suburbs. By the late 1990s, the percentage of Whites in the Aldine High student body had fallen from 50 percent to 15 percent over a decade. The loss of middle-class families of all races has had dramatic impacts on schools and other institutions. Marc Harris was a sophomore on the 1990 Aldine state championship team. He told me most of his high school teammates, whether Black or White, have left Aldine for outer suburbs where there is more space, less crime, and better schools. Harris has remained in Aldine because of his job as a captain with the Aldine Police Department.[4] Leaving Aldine was true of the former Aldine players I spoke with. Wide receiver Eric Stevens now lives in Spring, defensive back Larry Kissam lives in Humble, linebacker and fullback John Lacy lives in Klein, as do quarterback Eric Gray and left tackle Roderick Jordan. Steve Strahan also lives in Klein, where he is a teacher and an assistant football coach at Klein Forest High School. Offensive lineman Travis Coleman lives in The Woodlands, where he is an assistant football coach at College Park High School. In each case, the former Aldine players now reside in suburbs that are further from the city center, safer, and have better schools.

With the loss of middle-class families, both White and minority, many of the families remaining in Aldine are low income and nearly all are minority. In 2022, Aldine High was only 1.7 percent White. Over 90 percent of its students were on free or reduced lunch, and Aldine students averaged at the 11.4 percentile on standardized academic tests. In 2017, Children at Risk, a nonprofit organization seeking to improve educational opportunities for children, gave the school a grade of F. As is typical for low-income schools with virtually all minority students, the football team has experienced really hard times. In the ten years between 2013 and 2022, the Aldine Mustangs won a total of seven football games. In 2022, the football team finished the season with a record of 0–10 and were outscored 417–20 in district games. Not a single Aldine football player has been a top one hundred recruits since 2012. Summing up the current state of Aldine football, Larry Kissam from the 1990 championship team told me that for years there was a large sign on the interstate highway near the Aldine High campus. This sign listed all of the team's district championships, trips to the playoffs, and the 1990 state championship. In 2017, Hurricane Harvey blew the sign over. In the years since, no one has bothered to put the sign back up. Kissam said it was like history was being erased and nobody cared.

Schools in the inner ring of suburbs around Dallas are experiencing the same fate as Aldine. The suburb of Garland is located in the northeast corner of Dallas County. From early in the twentieth century, Garland was served by Garland High School. In later decades, Carver School was built for Black students living in Garland. Garland High won three state championships in the late 1950s and early 1960s. Due to its proximity to Dallas, Garland began to experience rapid growth around midcentury, and by 1964 a second high school was built in the city—South Garland High. In response to pressure to desegregate, Garland Independent School District implemented a freedom of choice plan in 1965. But then, seeing the writing on the wall, the district closed Carver School in 1967, and the Black students were distributed to the two White high schools in the city.

The Garland area grew especially rapidly during the 1970s, largely as a consequence of white flight as Dallas schools integrated. Other integrated schools in Garland ISD were built. During the 1970s and 1980s, Garland was a predominately White, middle-class suburb. In 1987, for example, 81.1 percent of the students at South Garland High were White. It was during this time that the school experienced its greatest success on the football field. In 1990 and 1991 combined, the South Garland High football team had a record of 18–5. In 1990, they lost to Dallas Carter in the second round of the playoffs by a score of 34–26.

Then in the 1990s, white flight reached Garland as White families
left for even more distant suburbs, and parts of Garland became largely
low-income minority neighborhoods. By 2022 only 4.3 percent of the
students at South Garland High were White, and 86.3 percent were
on free and reduced lunch. Like inner-city schools, many schools in
the inner ring of suburbs are doing poorly academically. Standardized
academic test scores for South Garland students averaged at the 11.4
percentile. The South Garland High football team is struggling as well.
In the ten years from 2013 to 2022, South Garland High won a total of
ten football games. In 2022, the team finished with a 1–9 record. Since
2012, South Garland has had one player who was a top one hundred
recruit. NBA basketball star Tyrese Maxey is from South Garland High.

The lone recent exception to the standard of inner-city school decline
was the back-to-back 5A state championships won by South Oak Cliff in
2021 and 2022. In many ways, the exception proves the rule. In winning
a state championship, South Oak Cliff became the first Dallas ISD team
to win a state championship since Dallas Carter's 1988 victory, a victory
that was later vacated due to violations of UIL player eligibility rules.
Prior to that, the last state champion from DISD was in 1950. The South
Oak Cliff championships were the only ones in the state since 2012 for
schools where over 90 percent of the students receive free or reduced
lunch. After struggling for several decades after Norman Jett was fired,
South Oak Cliff has benefited in recent years from excellent coaching.
Since 2015, the head coach had been Jason Todd, grandson of Frederick
Todd, the principal who fired Norman Jett. This has resulted in talented
players from throughout Dallas desiring to play at a school where they
can win and have a chance to be noticed by college recruiters.

Chris Gilbert graduated from South Oak Cliff in 1994, and then was
head football coach at the school from 2006–08. He told me that it took
exceptional coaching and a principal willing to try new ideas for the
school to turn the corner.[5] Gilbert is now an assistant football coach at
the University of North Texas. Between 2012 and 2021, ten South Oak
Cliff players were among the top one hundred recruits. Following the
2022 season, eleven South Oak Cliff players signed letters of intent with
four-year college programs. Among the top players were Malik Muhammad, who signed with the University of Texas, and Jayvon Thomas, who
signed with Texas A&M.

Socioeconomically Diverse Schools in
Medium-Sized Communities

With the success of high income, largely White suburban schools such as Southlake Carroll, Aledo, Katy, and Allen, along with the success of middle-class minority suburban schools such as North Shore, Duncanville, and DeSoto, the football success of schools in more racially and economically diverse suburbs and schools in medium-sized cities has declined. Odessa Permian and Temple, for example, continue to have competitive teams, but have never been able to repeat the success they experienced in the 1970s and 1980s. One school in this category that continued winning through the 1990s and into the early 2000s was Converse Judson. Converse is an economically and racially diverse suburban community near San Antonio. Demographically, the school resembles Odessa Permian or Temple. During the twenty-one-year period from 1982 to 2002, Converse Judson High School won 249 football games and six state championships—in 1983, 1988, 1992, 1993, 1995, and 2002. It should be noted that Judson actually lost the 1988 state championship game to Dallas Carter but was later awarded the championship trophy when Carter was declared ineligible as described earlier.

Like Permian and Temple, Converse Judson has experienced some success since their 2002 championship, but not at the level of previous decades. The approach that worked for Judson, Permian, and similar schools in previous decades is simply inadequate in the modern world. These schools continue to have strong community support, and devoted and talented coaches and players. The problem is the wealthy schools have everything the economically diverse schools have, plus other advantages that most Texas high school players simply cannot afford. These advantages include summer camps and private coaches. Occasionally, a school from this category will benefit from an extremely talented player or players to advance deep into the playoffs, and occasionally win it all, but such seasons are increasingly rare.[6]

Schools like Odessa Permian, Temple, and Converse Judson cannot seem to get by the likes of Southlake Carroll, Duncanville, North Shore, or Katy in the playoffs. Since the turn of the twenty-first century, Odessa Permian has never made it past the third round of the playoffs, the stage at which they typically play a suburban powerhouse from the Dallas-Fort

Worth metro area. In 2006, for example, Permian lost to Southlake Carroll 42–6. Two years later they lost to Allen, and in 2020 they again lost to Southlake Carroll. Permian, Temple, and similar schools are also not producing nearly as many highly recruited football players as schools in the more affluent suburbs. From 2012 to 2022, both Permian and Temple had three top one hundred recruits. The academic standing of these schools is also significantly lower than the wealthy suburban schools.

Similarly, the level of success of the schools in Beaumont has declined considerably. The city of Beaumont and Southeast Texas have a long and impressive football tradition. In earlier chapters of this book, the accomplishments of the city's segregated Black schools—Hebert and Charlton-Pollard—were discussed. Beaumont West Brook's state championship in 1982, the school's first year of existence following court-ordered integration has also been described. There was a time when, per capita, there were more players from Beaumont in the NFL than any other city in America.

Those days seem long gone. In 2022, there were two high schools in Beaumont, West Brook and United. As noted earlier, West Brook High School opened in 1982 following court-mandated integration and won a state championship in its first year of existence. Beaumont United High School was opened in 2018 as a result of the merger of Central High with Ozen High. Central High opened in 1986 to advance the integration efforts of Beaumont schools. Ozen High was opened in 1997 as a fine arts and technology magnet school and named after former Hebert High football coach Clifton Ozen. In 2017, Hurricane Harvey severely damaged the Central High campus. Rather than attempt to rebuild the school, the Central students were sent to Ozen, which was renamed United. In 2022, 17.5 percent of the students at West Brook High were White, 48.2 percent of students were on free and reduced lunch, and West Brook students on average scored at the 21.2 percentile on standardized academic scores. At United High, only 1.7 percent of the students were White, 81.8 percent were on free and reduced lunch, and their standardized academic scores were at the 7.5 percentile. From the low proportion of White students at the two high schools, it is clear Beaumont is experiencing white flight to surrounding communities such as Port Neches and Lumberton. A growing number of the White students living in Beaumont are also attending private schools.

Only a handful of 5A or 6A high schools in the entire state scored as bad or worse than Beaumont United High on standardized academic tests. All that did so were predominately minority schools where nearly everyone in the school was on free or reduced lunch. For example, students at Fort Worth Wyatt High scored at the 7.3 percentile on standardized tests; Wyatt High is only 3.2 percent White, and 96.4 percent of students are on free and reduced lunch. Laredo Cigarroa High is 100 percent Latino, and 97.6 percent of students receive free or reduced lunch. Cigarroa students on average scored at the 5.9 percentile on standardized tests.

Typical of predominately minority schools with low-income students, the West Brook and United football teams both struggled, and both finished the 2022 season with 1–9 records. West Brook's lone win was against United. United losses included a 69–0 defeat to Port Neches-Groves, 62–0 to North Shore, 55–0 to King, and 68–0 to Summer Creek. Darrell Colbert, who played on the 1982 West Brook state championship team, was in his first year as head coach at United in 2022. He is committed to bringing glory back to Beaumont football. His work is cut out for him if this is to be accomplished. He told me that he hopes to start by rebuilding the institutions that created so many great football players in the past, such as youth football. Rebuilding institutions such as youth football in low-income communities is difficult because of the lack of middle- and working-class people to do the work.[7]

The trajectory of Bryan High School is indicative of schools in this category of economically diverse schools in medium-sized cities. My family lived in Bryan for many years, and all of my children are graduates of Bryan High. As noted earlier, Bryan High was opened in 1971 with the merger of the White high school in the city (Stephen F. Austin) and the Black high school in the city (Kemp). The school had a number of solid football teams during the 1970s, 1980s, and 1990s. My son was the starting center on the 1999 team that advanced deep in the playoffs. Bryan High has produced several exceptional football players including Curtis Dickey, Rod Bernstine, and Ty Warren. All three attended nearby Texas A&M after graduating from Bryan High. Dickey was selected in the first round of the 1980 NFL draft, Bernstine in the first round of the 1987 draft, and Warren in the first round of the 2003 draft. Warren won two Super Bowl rings while playing defensive tackle for the New England Patriots. For many years, Bryan had the misfortune of being in the same district as Temple. Three times in the 1970s, Bryan finished the year with a 9–1 record but failed to make the playoffs. Each time the one loss was to Temple, and that loss cost them the district championship and a chance for the playoffs. This was during the era when only the district champion advanced to the playoffs.

Bryan is also adjacent to College Station, home of Texas A&M University. While my kids were growing up, each city had one high school—A&M Consolidated High in College Station and Bryan High in Bryan. With steady growth, each community has recently opened a second high school—College Station High in College Station and Rudder High in Bryan. In recent years, the fortunes of schools in Bryan relative to College Station have gone in different directions. College Station schools have always had a higher proportion of White students compared to Bryan. In recent years, the economic gap between the two cities has grown as Texas A&M faculty and administrators and other professionals in the community have increasingly chosen to live in College Station as opposed to Bryan. The racial and economic differences between the cities and their schools are now rather large. This makes Bryan a more difficult place to teach and coach.[8] The high schools in College Station are now similar to other wealthy suburban schools, while Bryan schools are more similar to those in other socioeconomically diverse medium-sized cities. In the two College Station high schools, the percentage of students on free and reduced lunch are 27.5 and 30.5 percent; their average score on standardized academic tests are 79.9 and 78.8 percent. In comparison, in Bryan, the percentage of students on free and reduced lunch are 64.7 and 74.5 percent, while average scores on standardized academic tests are 27 and 16.2 percent. The differences are now evident on the football field. College Station High School opened in 2014. Three years later, in 2017, College Station High won a 5A state championship in football by defeating Aledo. In 2021 they lost in the state championship game, and in 2022 they again advanced to the state championship game and lost to Aledo.

Smaller Texas High Schools

The focus of the last few chapters has been on larger high schools in the state. In many ways, change toward resegregation has been less apparent in high schools in smaller communities around the state. In Brownwood, for example, all students in the city, regardless of race, attend the same school, as they have done since integration in the 1950s. Changes in the racial composition of schools are simply a consequence of demographic changes in the community. In Brownwood High, for example, the percentage of students who are Black has remained very consistent since integration. The percent of students who are Hispanic has increased rapidly in recent decades, with a corresponding decline in the percentage of White students.

As a result, the extent to which some schools have structural advantages over other schools is much less among smaller schools like Brownwood compared to larger schools in the big cities. The schools that win championships are those with a group of talented players passing through and talented coaches to develop their skills. Consequently, the same few schools don't dominate the state playoffs to the extent they do among the large schools. At Brownwood and other smaller schools, nearly all players on the varsity team played on the school's seventh grade team a few years ago. Few people move to isolated small towns to play football, and so the recruiting of players from other schools generally does not occur.

The current head football coach at Brownwood is Sammy Burnett. Coach Burnett grew up in Brownwood, played for the Brownwood Lions, and fulfilled a lifetime dream when he was hired as the head coach of his hometown team. Coach Gordon Wood retired in 1985 following Coach Burnett's sophomore year in high school. Burnett's goal is to teach the kids who play for him the value of setting goals, working hard, and teamwork. His dream and the dream of the community is that someday they will win state championship number eight to add to the seven won by Coach Wood.[9]

Playoff Results in 2022 for the Different Categories of High Schools

The depth of inequality in Texas high schools is apparent by looking at the 2022 Texas high school football playoffs. Again, there are four state championships awarded at the 5A and 6A levels, all based on school enrollment. When the playoffs began, there were sixty-four teams in each classification, which means 256 teams across 5A and 6A made the playoffs. This was just over half of the 498 schools that participated in the 5A and 6A classifications that year. Advantaged schools were more likely to make the playoffs. Sixty-nine percent of schools where 10 percent or less of the students received free or reduced lunch made the playoffs, while this proportion declined to 29 percent for schools where 90 percent or more of students received free or reduced lunch.

When each classification had reached its final four, a total of sixteen schools remained. Of these teams that had survived four rounds of playoffs, eleven could be defined as wealthy suburban schools. Included in this group were traditional powers such as Katy, Aledo, and Austin Westlake. Other wealthy suburban schools advanced deep in the playoffs before falling. The Southlake Carroll Dragons finished the regular season with a perfect 10–0 record. Included were wins over Cedar Hill 47–6; Fort Worth Timber Creek 51–0; Haltom 62–0; and Keller Central 49–3. In their first playoff game, the Dragons defeated Crowley 52–13. This was followed by wins over Wolfforth Frenship 69–14 and McKinney 42–35. The Dragons were then defeated by Denton Guyer 45–21. Guyer, another wealthy suburban school, entered the game against Southlake Carroll undefeated and ranked number one in the state. Guyer was led by Jackson Arnold, one of the top high school quarterbacks in the nation and a University of Oklahoma commit. Highland Park also entered the 2022 playoffs undefeated but had the misfortune of playing Denton Guyer in the second round and were beaten.

Three more of the schools that advanced to the final four in their divisions were predominately minority, middle-class, suburban schools, including powerful programs at Duncanville, DeSoto, and Galena Park North Shore. Duncanville entered the playoffs undefeated. Through the first five rounds of the playoffs, only one team came within thirty points of them. Similarly, North Shore cruised through four rounds of playoffs. In the state semifinals, North Shore ended the fifty-four-game winning streak of Austin Westlake and then met Duncanville in a titanic battle of unbeaten teams for the 6A Division I state championship. This was the fourth time the two programs met in the state championship since 2017. North Shore won the first three meetings, including in 2018 when North Shore won the game on a last-play Hail Mary pass. In 2022, Duncanville was finally able to beat North Shore by a score of 28–21.

DeSoto is in the same district as Duncanville and finished in second place in the district with its only district loss coming at the hands of Duncanville by a score of 41–17. DeSoto had fewer students than Duncanville, and so competed in 6A Division II. They rolled through four rounds of playoffs and then met top-ranked Denton Guyer in the semifinals. DeSoto was victorious by a score of 47–28. DeSoto's opponent in the championship game was Vandegrift High, a wealthy suburban school on the west side of Austin that opened its doors in 2010. Vandegrift made it to the state championship game with a 38–35 win over undefeated Katy in the semifinals. Vandegrift hit a thirty-seven-yard field goal on the game's final play for the dramatic win. In the championship game, DeSoto defeated Vandegrift 42–17.

In comparison, socioeconomically diverse schools in medium-sized sized cities did not fare nearly as well. Odessa Permian High finished the 2022 regular season with a 9–1 record, and in a three-way tie for the district championship. Their only loss was by a 33–25 score to their traditional rival Midland Legacy (formerly Midland Lee). In the first round of the playoffs, Permian was defeated by El Paso Pebble Hills 45–28. Permian often plays a team from El Paso in the first or second round of the playoffs. Up until 2022, Permian had lost this game only once—in 2012—since 1960. Bryan entered the playoffs with a 6–4 record and was crushed by Duncanville 74–13 in the first round. Temple earned a trip to the playoffs with a 7–3 record, while Converse Judson earned a playoff spot with a 4–6 record. Temple lost its first playoff game, while Converse Judson won its first playoff game before losing. The only school in this category to advance deeply in the playoffs was Longview. Longview won the state championship in 2018. In 2022 it lost in the state semifinals to Aledo 17–14. Aledo went on to beat College Station in the championship game to earn its tenth state championship since 2009.

Inner-city and inner-suburban schools also fared poorly in the 2022 playoffs. Because of reduced enrollment, most inner-city schools competed at smaller classifications. Carter completed the regular season with a record of 8–2. Competing in the 4A playoffs, Carter won its first game but lost in the second round. Yates made the playoffs with a 5–5 record and then lost its first playoff game to Bay City by a score of 57–0. Kashmere finished the regular season with a 3–7 record and failed to make the playoffs. Aldine and South Garland won only one game combined, and neither made the playoffs. Again, the lone exception was Dallas South Oak Cliff, which earned its second consecutive state championship in 2022.

Among the smaller schools, Brownwood finished the regular season with an 8–2 record and the district championship. The Lions won their first two playoff games before falling to Wichita Falls in the third round. As noted earlier, among smaller schools, domination by the same school over long periods of time is less likely to occur than among large city schools.

Epilogue

In 1954 Texas high schools were separate and unequal. While progress was made in the decades immediately following the 1954 *Brown* decision, by the 1970s integration efforts had largely been abandoned and resegregation began. Now, seventy years after *Brown*, Texas high schools are again separate and very unequal. Just as in 1954, most White kids are attending quality high schools where they can get an excellent education and have the chance to participate in exceptional extracurricular activities, including football. Not only do students in economically advantaged schools do better academically, but these schools also win more football games, win more football state championships, and produce more highly recruited football players.

Critically, economic advantage intersects closely with race. As a result, for the majority of Black and Hispanic students, things are very much like they were seventy years ago; they are attending inferior schools with limited resources and limited educational and extracurricular opportunities. A miniscule percentage of their classmates are White, and nearly all of their fellow students come from poor families.

Seventy years ago, the law required separate schools. School segregation is no longer the law, and today, the line separating students is not as precise as it was in the 1950s. Today there are some minority students attending high quality schools and most of their classmates are White. In most cases, these minority kids are at least middle class and can afford to live in the affluent neighborhoods that feed these top schools. Yet today, thousands of low-income minority kids are attending what are in effect, segregated schools. As Rucker C. Johnson, an economist at University of California, Berkeley, stated, "No one is throwing rocks at buses carrying black kids to white schools anymore, largely because those buses are no longer running."[1]

It is important to remember that there is nothing magic about sitting next to a White kid in class. Rather, most schools with significant numbers of students from advantaged families tend to have a high proportion of White students. Attending a school with advantaged students helps people become aware of the realm of possibilities available to them. Advantaged schools typically have better facilities and more accomplished teachers. Also, low-income students of all races do better in socioeconomically mixed schools than in schools where most of their peers are from low-income homes. Another problem with economically segregated schools is that middle-class students of all races do poorly in schools where most of their fellow students are poor.

There are many reasons why schools with large numbers of low-income students struggle compared to advantaged schools. Many advantaged students come from homes and communities that provide experiences that pave the way for success in school. Typically, advantaged students live in homes with books and computers. Their behavior generally reflects the widely shared, high-status cultural signals that are recognized and appreciated by teachers. These cultural signals tend to be learned through activities such as theater, museum attendance, literature, and travel— activities often unavailable to students from low-income families.

Additionally, many low-income students come from unstable families, and a significant proportion of them come from single-parent homes. Many children from low-income families and neighborhoods lack examples of how to achieve success. Trauma in the lives of kids from low-income homes is all too common. Traumatic events include observing or being the victim of violence, family breakups, hunger, and severe uncertainty about the future. Young people who have experienced trauma are much more likely to misbehave in school and elsewhere. These factors combined mean that many teachers find working in advantaged schools to be easier and more rewarding than working in disadvantaged schools where misbehavior is more common. Further, because advantaged districts are likely to have more resources, teachers tend to earn higher wages. As a result, teachers in low-income schools often seek after and will jump at the chance to take a job with a more advantaged school.

Whether a student attends an advantaged or disadvantaged school has dramatic consequences for his or her life chances after high school.

When schools are separate and unequal, the education system quickly becomes a tool for advantaged families to secure and maintain socially advantaged positions for themselves and their children.[2] Students attending advantaged schools score better on standardized tests, get admitted to better colleges, are more likely to graduate from college, and have more success later in life. The benefits of attending advantaged schools extend to students from disadvantaged families. Research shows that disadvantaged students who attend advantaged schools do better than their similarly disadvantaged peers who are attending disadvantaged schools.[3] Today, thousands of minority and low-income students are largely unaware of the daily lives of middle- and upper-class Americans. At the same time, thousands of middle- and upper-class students are largely unaware of the world that students in disadvantaged schools live in. I am convinced that society would greatly benefit if both were aware of conditions on the other side of the tracks.

In critically significant ways, the schools in which nearly all of the students are both poor and minority are worse off than the segregated schools prior to *Brown*. Prior to integration, virtually all minority families were forced to live in select neighborhoods in cities because of redlining and other discriminatory policies. As Bob Kenrick, president of the Negro Leagues Baseball Museum, has said, speaking from the perspective of Blacks living in legally segregated America, "It didn't matter how much money Satchel Page, Buck O'Neil, Josh Gibson, Cool Papa Bell made, they lived in the same neighborhood that I lived in. I saw them virtually every day. We worshipped in the same place, we went to the same barbershop, we were eating in the same segregated restaurants.[4] What was true of pro athletes was true of teachers, doctors, lawyers, and business owners. As a result, the middle- and working-class individuals residing in these minority communities were critical in helping important institutions, such as schools, run efficiently. These people also provided examples and were mentors to young people during a time in life when these kids made important decisions that would largely determine their futures. With the removal of discriminatory housing policies, most of these individuals no longer reside in disadvantaged communities, having moved to suburbs that are safer and have better schools.

Attending an advantaged school not only provides extensive benefits in the classroom, it also makes it possible for students to participate in high quality extracurricular activities, such as football. The benefits to students of being a part of a high quality football program are extensive. Of course, many of these same benefits can also be obtained by participating in other quality school activities. Extensive research has found that high school students who play sports—whether it be football, golf, tennis, or anything else—or play in the band, sing in the choir, or participate on the debate team, have better grades, score higher on standardized tests, are less likely to drop out of school, have reduced alcohol or drug use, and have greater educational attainment levels later in life.[5] Legendary women's basketball coach Gary Blair stated, "What inspires me is that basketball can be used to build foundations for future success. What motivates me is the concept that victories and defeats, trials and triumphs, and adversities and accomplishments can teach life lessons that will be applicable to my players long after their basketball careers have ended."[6] Many of the high school coaches I interviewed recognized that only a small proportion of the players they coach will ever play football beyond high school. Consequently, they emphasize teaching skills and values that will last a lifetime, such as commitment, working hard to achieve a goal, and working together as a team.

The comradery that develops among teammates can result in bonds that last a lifetime. Playing side by side with someone of a different race or social class than you tends to tear down stereotypes and reduces prejudice. Interaction with coaches often has positive influences on the choices students make. High school football can create community cohesion and build community pride. Beyond all of this, for a teenager to be a part of the atmosphere that is Texas high school football with the cheering crowds, the cheerleaders, and the band, all provides an adrenaline rush that for many will seldom be reached again the rest of their lives. Eric Dickerson was a college all-American and an NFL Hall of Famer. He played before packed stadiums with millions of people watching on TV. Yet he says that playing high school football in Sealy, Texas was the greatest experience of his life. For him, high school football was fun and less of the business that football became later in life. In addition, in high school he was playing with kids he had grown up with and known all his life.[7]

Marcus Allen provides a graphic example of the potential benefits from attending a good high school and playing on a quality high school

football team. Allen was a member of the 1990 Aldine state championship team. The first time I talked to Allen he was in an Uber on his way
home from the airport after a business trip to Boston. He works for a
Kuwait-based equity investment firm in the management of its health
care division. He has a master's degree and earns a substantial income.
He told me about his feeling of euphoria the first time he was handed a
paycheck for $30,000.

Things were not always that way for Marcus Allen. He grew up in the
Garden City Apartments, low-income projects that are one of the roughest places in Acres Homes, which is one of the roughest neighborhoods
in Houston. Allen told me his single-parent mother did the best she
could. She wanted to raise her son in a better, safer place, but she simply
didn't have the money to get out of the projects. Like other kids from
Garden City, he sometimes went to school hungry. Football helped him
become aware of the larger world. Football then opened the door to an
education that allowed him to escape from poverty. After high school,
Allen was heavily recruited to play college football. He told me that some
of the coaches recruiting him were afraid to come into the apartment
complex where he lived. The first time Allen ever got on an airplane was
on a football recruiting trip. He eventually chose to attend college and
play football for TCU. Because of his background, he was unprepared for
college and the classwork was difficult for him at first. But he persevered
and worked hard. He is innately bright, and all he needed was a chance.
After graduating from TCU, he went on to earn a master's degree, and
the rest is history. Those who know Allen say that he is a great dad and
tries to be the father to his children that he never had.

In the unequal school system of today, the benefits accrued to individuals and communities from high school football vary greatly. The same
is true of other extracurricular activities as well as academics. At some
high schools, the kids get to play football in front of large crowds; at
other schools, the crowds are sparse. Some schools can afford to hire the
best coaches; others can't. Some kids see benefits from their hard work;
others don't. Some schools develop students in academics, athletics, and
other skills, which helps them earn scholarships and be admitted to top
universities; others don't.

In 1990, Marcus Allen played for a state championship program. He
learned hard work, consistency, teamwork, and excellence. He learned

that when allowed to compete on a level playing field, he had the ability, intelligence, and grit to beat anyone in the state, and this experience opened doors of opportunity and changed his life. But what if Marcus Allen had been born a generation later? A poor Black kid with a single mother growing up Acres Homes in 2023 would attend an underfunded failing school where 98 percent of students are minority and 90 percent are economically disadvantaged. If he played football, he would play for a team that has lost thirty-four games in a row, regularly losing by fifty, sixty, or seventy points. Would he develop his talents? Would anybody notice? Does anyone care?

Notes

Prologue

1. Harold B. Gerard and Norman Miller, *School Desegregation: A Long-Term Study* (New York: Springer Science & Business Media, 2013).

2. Kriston McIntosh, Emily Moss, Ryan Nunn, and Jay Shambaugh, "Examining the Black-white Wealth Gap," *Brookings Institution.* February 27, 2020, https://www .brookings.edu/articles/examining-the-black-white-wealth-gap/.

3. Jeremy Travis, Bruce Western, and F. Stevens Redburn, *The Growth of Incarceration in the United States: Exploring Causes and Consequences* (New York: National Academies Press, 2014).

4. Ramona Houston "'Wicked Policing:' A Reality in all Black Communities Throughout America." (blog), *RamonaHouston.com*, January 29, 2023. https://ramona houston.com/social-impact-social-responsibility/wicked-policing-a-reality-in-all-black-communities-throughout-america/.

Chapter One

1. Henry Louis Gates Jr., *Stony the Road* (New York: Penguin, 2014).

2. Eric Dickerson and Greg Hanlan, *Watch my Smoke* (Chicago: Haymaker Books, 2022).

3. James MacGregor Burns and Jack Walter Peltason, *Government by the People* (Englewood Cliffs, NJ: Prentice-Hall, 1969)

4. Roger A. Fisher, *The Segregation Struggle in Louisiana, 1862–1877* (Urbana: University of Illinois Press, 1974).

5. C. Vann Woodward, *The Strange Career of Jim Crow* (New York: Oxford University Press, 1955).

6. Burns and Peltason, *Government by the People*, 157.

7. Fisher, *The Segregation Struggle in Louisiana*.

8. Fisher, *The Segregation Struggle in Louisiana*.

9. Dickerson and Hanlan, *Watch my Smoke*.

10. Gunnar Myrdal, *An American Dilemma: The Negro Problem and Modern Democracy* (New York: McGraw-Hill, 1962): Page 205.

11. James P. Smith and Finis R. Welch, *Closing the Gap: Forty Years of Economic Progress for Blacks* (Santa Monica, CA: The Rand Corporation, 1986).

12. Isabel Wilkerson, *The Warmth of other Suns: The Epic Story of America's Great Migration* (London: Penguin, 2020).

13. *Dallas Morning News*, December 30, 1945.

14. *Dallas Morning News*, January 2, 1946.

15. Michael Hurd, *Thursday Night Lights* (Austin: University of Texas Press, 2017).

16. *Houston Post*, November 21, 1945.

17. Gilbert Osofsky, *The Burden of Race: A Documentary History of Negro-White Relations in America* (New York: Harper and Row, 1945).

18. Jules Tygiel, *Baseball's Great Experiment: Jackie Robinson and his Legacy* (New York: Oxford University Press, 1983).

19. Adrian Burgos Jr., *Playing America's Game: Baseball, Latinos, and the Color Line* (Berkley: University of California Press, 2007).

20. Tygiel, *Baseball's Great Experiment.*

21. Tygiel, *Baseball's Great Experiment, 24.*

22. Tygiel, *Baseball's Great Experiment.*

23. Tygiel, *Baseball's Great Experiment.*

24. Letter from Yankee President Larry MacPhail to New York Mayor Laguardia, 1945.

25. Tygiel, *Baseball's Great Experiment.*

26. Tygiel, *Baseball's Great Experiment.*

27. Charles H. Martin, *Benching Jim Crow* (Urbana: University of Illinois Press, 2020).

28. Richard Pennington, *Breaking the Ice: The Racial Integration of Southwest Conference Football* (Jefferson, NC: McFarland and Co., Inc. 1987).

29. Pennington, *Breaking the Ice.*

Chapter Two

1. Raymond Wolters, *The Burden of Brown: Thirty Years of School Desegregation* (Knoxville: The University of Tennessee Press, 1984).

2. Robert Jacobus, *Black Man in the Huddle* (College Station: Texas A&M University Press, 2019).

3. *Southern School News*, May 17, 1964.

4. Charles T. Clotfelter, *After Brown: The Rise and Retreat of School Desegregation* (Princeton, NJ: Princeton University Press, 2004).

5. *Houston Informer*, August 1954.

6. Robyn Duff Ladino, *Desegregating Texas Schools* (Austin: University of Texas Press, 1996): 5.

7. Ladino, *Desegregating Texas Schools.*

8. *Southern School News*, May 17, 1964.

9. Ladino, *Desegregating Texas Schools.*

10. Ladino, *Desegregating Texas Schools.*

11. *Southern School News*, May 17, 1964.

12. H. G. Bissinger, *Friday Night Lights* (New York: Da Capo Press, 1990).

13. William Henry Kellar, *Make Haste Slowly: Moderates, Conservatives and School Desegregation in Houston* (College Station: Texas A&M University Press, 1999).

14. Kellar, *Make Haste Slowly.*

15. *Southern School News*, May 17, 1964.

Chapter Three

1. Bissinger, *Friday Night Lights.*

2. Jeff Fisher, *High School Football in Texas: Amazing Football Stories for the Greatest Players of Texas* (New York: Sports Publishing, 2018).

3. Bill McMurray, *Texas High School Football* (South Bend, Indiana: Icarus Press, 1985).

4. Harold Ratliff, *Autumn's Mightiest Legions: History of Texas Schoolboy Football* (Waco: Texian Press, 1963).

5. Ratliff, *Autumn's Mightiest Legions.*

6. Derral Hill Elmore, *History of Texas Interscholastic League of Colored Schools* (M.S. Thesis, Prairie View A&M University, 1985).

7. Elmore, *History of Texas Interscholastic League of Colored Schools.*

8. McMurray, *Texas High School Football.*

9. Oland Rogers (head football coach at Douglass High School, the segregated Black high school in Pittsburg, Texas), interviewed by the author, 1991.

10. *Dallas Morning News*, September 1989.

Chapter Four

1. W. N. Corder (principal at Robstown High starting in 1949 and including integration in 1955), interviewed by the author, 1991.

2. Robert (Bobby) Goff (coached high school football at Yoakum High in 1955 and later coached at Goliad High and Calhoun High in Port Lavaca), interviewed by the author, 1991.

3. Billie Jean Pogue Goff (married Bobby Goff on December 7, 1946; married for sixty years and had three daughters), interviewed by the author, 1991.

4. *Dave Campbell's Texas Football*, 1976.

5. Jacobus, *Black Man in the Huddle.*

6. Gordon Wood (Texas high school football coach for forty-three years, including twenty-six at Brownwood High), interviewed by the author, 1991.

7. Cecil Houston (football player for Gordon Wood at Brownwood High in the early 1960s and father of Ramona Houston), interviewed by the author, 1991.

8. Dr. Ramona Houston (daughter of Cecil Houston), interviewed by the author, February 13, 2022.

9. Junior Coffey (attended high school in Dimmit and played college football at Washington and in the NFL with the Green Bay Packers), interviewed by the author, 1991.

10. Beral Hance (Dimmit resident and mother of Kent Hance; taught at the segregated Black school in during the 1950s), interviewed by the author, 1991.

11. Kent Hance (grew up in Dimmit and was friends and teammates with Junior Coffey; elected to US Congress and later served as chancellor of the Texas Tech University System), interviewed by the author, 1991.

12. *Dallas Morning News*, December 1962.

13. *The Best of Dave Campbell's Texas Football*, 1989.

14. Art Delgado (player on the 1958 Corpus Christi Miller High state championship team), interviewed by the author, 1991.

15. *Dallas Morning News*, December 16, 1959.

16. Pennington, *Breaking the Ice*.

17. *The Best of Dave Campbell's Texas Football*, 1989.

18. Willie Ray Smith (Beaumont area football coach), interviewed by the author, 1990.

19. Clifton Ozen (Beaumont Hebert High School football coach), interviewed by the author, 1990.

20. Hurd, *Thursday Night Lights*.

21. Hurd, *Thursday Night Lights*.

22. Hurd, *Thursday Night Lights*.

23. Hurd, *Thursday Night Lights*, 54.

Chapter Five

1. National Advisory Commission on Civil Disorders, *Kerner Commission Report on the Causes, Events, and Aftermaths of the Civil Disorders of 1967*, 1968, US National Institute of Justice.

2. Jerry Honore (Lake Charles, Louisiana, native and first Black scholarship football player at Texas A&M), interviewed by the author, October 27, 2022.

3. Hurd, *Thursday Night Lights*.

4. *Houston Post*, November 23, 1966.

5. *Dave Campbell's Texas Football*, 1967.

6. Luther Booker (head football coach at Yates High School for eighteen years), interviewed by the author, 1990.

7. Ozen, interview.

8. Paul Register (Texas high school football coach and long-time assistant football coach at Texas A&M University), interviewed by the author, 1991.

9. Pennington, *Breaking the Ice*

10. Pennington, *Breaking the Ice*.

11. J. T. Reynolds (1968 walk-on and first Black player to appear in a game for the Texas A&M Aggies), interviewed by the author, 1991.

12. Sammy Williams, (1968 walk-on for Texas A&M football team and second Black player to appear in a game for the Aggies), interviewed by the author, 1991.

13. Hugh McElroy, (first Black player to start a game and score a touchdown for Texas A&M), interviewed by the author, 1991.

Chapter Six

1. Charles T. Clotfelter, *After Brown: The Rise and Retreat of School Desegregation* (Princeton, NJ: Princeton University Press, 2004).

2. Hurd, *Thursday Night Lights*, 49.

3. Reynolds Farley, Sheldon Danziger, and Harry J. Holzer, *Detroit Divided* (New York: Russell Sage Foundation, 2000).

4. Matthew Delmont, *Why Busing Failed* (Oakland: University of California Press, 2016).

5. Delmont, *Why Busing Failed*.

6. Rosa Parks, *Cradle of the Confederacy Letters*. Rosa Parks Collection, Library of Congress, Box 18, Folder 10, 1957.

7. Michael O'Brien, *Hesburgh: A Biography*. (Washington, DC: Catholic University of America Press, 1998).

8. Delmont, *Why Busing Failed*.

9. R. C. Slocum (Texas A&M assistant football coach 1972–88 and head football coach 1989–2002; holds program record for wins with 123), interviewed by the author, October 27, 2022.

10. Earnest (Bubba) Bean (player at Kirbyville, Texas A&M from 1972–75, and Atlanta Falcons), interviewed by the author, February 20, 2023.

11. Hurd, *Thursday Night Lights*, 40.

12. Dickerson and Hanlan, *Watch my Smoke*.

Chapter Seven

1. Bissinger, *Friday Night Lights*.

2. *ESPN 30 for 30*, "What Carter Lost," directed by Adam Hootnick, documentary released August 24, 2017.

3. Greg Hill (running back at Dallas Carter, Texas &M, and Kansas City Chiefs; NFL first round draft choice in 1994), interviewed by the author, September 9, 2022.

4. Barbara Brown McCoy (basketball player at South Oak Cliff, Stephen F. Austin, US Pan American, and Olympic teams), interviewed by the author, November 16, 2022.

5. Gary Blair (girls' basketball coach South Oak Cliff High School and Texas A&M), interviewed by the author, November 14, 2022.

6. Darrell Colbert (football player at Beaumont Hebert High, Beaumont West Brook, Texas Southern, and Kansas City Chiefs; head coach at Beaumont United High School), interviewed by the author, October 18, 2022.

7. Bill Smith (head football coach at Aldine High 1975–2003), interviewed by the author, November 30, 2022.

8. Robert Gipson (football player at Aldine Carver High, Aldine High, and Baylor), interviewed by the author, November 18, 2022.

9. Pat Patterson (defensive coordinator on the 1990 Aldine state championship team, head coach at Aldine Eisenhower and Tomball for sixteen years), interviewed by the author, November 22, 2022.

10. Bissinger, *Friday Night Lights,*

11. Steve Strahan (defensive lineman for Aldine High 1990 state champions and at Baylor), interviewed by the author, November 22, 2022.

12. Eric Gray (quarterback for Aldine High 1990 state champions), interviewed by the author, November 19, 2022.

13. Travis Coleman (offensive lineman for Aldine High 1990 state champions) interviewed by the author, November 28, 2022.

14. Roderick Jordan (offensive lineman for Aldine High 1990 state champions), interviewed by the author, November 28, 2022.

15. Tremel Prudhomme (offensive lineman for Aldine High 1990 state champions), interviewed by the author, November 28, 2022.

16. Eric Stevens (wide receiver for the 1990 Aldine High state champions), interviewed by the author, November 29, 2022.

17. Marcus Allen (linebacker for the 1990 Aldine High state champions), interviewed by the author, November 17, 2022.

18. John Lacy (linebacker and fullback for Aldine High 1990 state champions), interviewed by the author, November 20, 2022.

19. Larry Kissam (defensive back for Aldine High 1990 state champions), interviewed by the author, November 30, 2022.

20. Bissinger, *Friday Night Lights.*

21. Bissinger, *Friday Night Lights.*

22. Rick Sherrod, *Texas High School Football Dynasties* (Charleston, SC: The History Press, 2013).

Chapter Eight

1. Michelle Alexander, *The New Jim Crow: Mass Incarceration in the Age of Color Blindness* (New York: The New Press, 2010).

2. Wesley Lowery, *They Can't Kill Us All* (New York: Little, Brown and Company, 2010).

3. Charles T. Clotfelter, *After Brown: The Rise and Retreat of School Desegregation* (Princeton, NJ: Princeton University Press, 2004).

4. S. F. Reardon and A. Owens, "60 years after Brown: Trends and Consequences of School Segregation," *Annual Review of Sociology* 40, no. 1 (2014): 199–218.

5. Gary Orfield and Erica Frankenberg, "Increasingly Segregated and Unequal School as Courts Reverse Policy," *Educational Administration Policy* 50, no. 5 (2014): 718–734.

6. Kiana Cox and Khadijah Edwards, "Black Americans Have a Clear Vision for Reducing Racism but Little Hope it Will Happen," *Pew Research Center*, August 30, 2022.

7. D. H. Autor, L. F. Katz, and M. S. Kearney, "Trends in US Wage Inequality: Revising the Revisionists," *The Review of Economics and Statistics* 90, no. 2 (2008): 300–323.

Chapter Nine

1. J. E. Fiel, "Decomposing School Resegregation: Social Closure, Racial Imbalance, and Racial Isolation," *American Sociological Review* 78, no. 5 (2013): 828–848.

2. Alana Semuals, "The Utter Inadequacy of America's Efforts to Desegregate School," *Atlantic*, April 11, 2019.

Chapter Ten

1. Tim Buchanan (won eight state championships during twenty-five-year Aledo High School head football coach tenure and three state championships in five-year tenure as athletic director), interviewed by the author, April 13, 2023.

2. Sherrod, *Texas High School Football Dynasties.*

3. Jacob Green (played for Kashmere High, Texas A&M, and the Seattle Seahawks), interviewed by the author, October 28, 2022.

4. Marcus Harris (sophomore on the 1990 Aldine High state championship team, became a captain on the Aldine Police Department), interviewed by the author, November 18, 2022.

5. Chris Gilbert (graduated from and coached at South Oak Cliff High School, became assistant head coach and tight end coach at North Texas State University), interviewed by the author, July 20, 2023.

6. Craig Stump (quarterback at Port Arthur Jefferson High and then Texas A&M University, became head football coach at Atascocita High School in 2012), interviewed by the author, January 11, 2023.

7. Colbert, interview.

8. Eric Eike (former teacher and coach at Bryan High School), interviewed by the author, July 19, 2023.

9. Sammy Burnett (Brownwood High player who became his alma mater's head coach in 2018), interviewed by the author, January 13, 2023.

Epilogue

1. Rucker C. Johnson, *Children of the Dream: Why School Integration Works* (New York: Basic Books, 2019).

2. Carol Mulford Albrecht and Don E. Albrecht, "Social Status, Adolescent Behavior, and Educational Attainment," *Sociological Spectrum* 31, no. 1 (2010): 114–137.

3. Will Dobbie and Roland G. Fryer Jr., "The Impact of Attending a School with High-Achieving Peers: Evidence from the New York City Exam Schools," *American Economic Journal: Applied Economics* 6, no. 3 (2014): 58–75.

4. Bob Kendrick, "Curtis Granderson and Edwin Jackson," produced by Bob Kendrick. *Black Diamonds*, July 20, 2023, https://black-diamonds.simplecast.com/episodes/curtis-granderson-and-edwin-jackson-the-players-alliance-recorded-at-all-star-week-in-seattle.

5. Beckett A. Broh, "Linking Extracurricular Programming to Academic Achievement: Who Benefits and Why," *Sociology of Education* 75, no. 1 (2002): 69–95.

6. Gary Blair and Rusty Berson, *A Coaching Life* (College Station: Texas A&M University Press, 2017).

7. Dickerson and Hanlan, *Watch my Smoke.*

Bibliography

Albrecht, Carol Mulford, and Don E. Albrecht. "Social Status, Adolescent Behavior, and Educational Attainment." *Sociological Spectrum* 31, no. 1 (2010): 114–37.

Alexander, Michelle. *The New Jim Crow: Mass Incarceration in the Age of Color Blindness*. New York: The New Press, 2010.

Autor, D. H., L. F. Katz, and M. S. Kearney. "Trends in US Wage inequality: Revising the Revisionists." *The Review of Economics and Statistics* 90, no. 2 (2008): 300–23.

Bissinger, H. G. *Friday Night Lights*. Philadelphia: Da Capo Press, 1990.

Blair, Gary, and Rusty Berson. *A Coaching Life*. College Station: Texas A&M University Press, 2017.

Broh, Beckett A. "Linking Extracurricular Programming to Academic Achievement: Who Benefits and Why." *Sociology of Education* 75, no. 1 (2002): 69–95.

Burgos, Adrian, and Adrian Jr. Burgos. *Playing America's Game: Baseball, Latinos, and the Color Line*, Berkley: University of California Press, 2007.

Burns, James MacGregor, and Jack Walter Peltason. *Government by the People*. Englewood Cliffs, NJ: Prentice-Hall, 1969.

Clotfelter, Charles T. *After Brown: The Rise and Retreat of School Desegregation*. Princeton, NJ: Princeton University Press, 2004.

Cox, Kiana, and Khadijah Edwards. "Black Americans Have a Clear Vision for Reducing Racism but Little Hope it Will Happen." *Pew Research Center*, August 30, 2022.

Delmont, Matthew F. "Why Busing Failed." Oakland: University of California Press, 2016.

Dickerson, Eric, and Greg Hanlan. *Watch my Smoke*. Chicago: Haymaker Books, 2022.

Dobbie, Will, and Roland G. Fryer Jr. "The Impact of Attending a School with High-Achieving Peers: Evidence from the New York City Exam Schools." *American Economic Journal: Applied Economics* 6, no. 3 (2014): 58–75.

Elmore, Derral Hill. *History of Texas Interscholastic League of Colored Schools*. M.S. Thesis, Prairie View A&M University, 1969.

Farley, Reynolds, Sheldon Danziger, and Harry J. Holzer. *Detroit Divided*. New York: Russell Sage Foundation, 2000.

Fiel, J. E. "Decomposing School Resegregation: Social Closure, Racial Imbalance, and Racial Isolation." *American Sociological Review* 78, no. 5 (2013): 828–48.

Fisher, Jeff. *High School Football in Texas: Amazing Football Stories for the Greatest Players of Texas*. New York: Sports Publishing, 2018.

Fisher, Roger A. *The Segregation Struggle in Louisiana, 1862–1877*. Urbana: University of Illinois Press, 1974.

Gates, Henry Louis Jr. *Stony the Road*. New York: Penguin, 2019.

Gerard, H. *School Desegregation: A Long-Term Study*. New York: Springer Science & Business Media, 2013.

Houston, Ramona. "'Wicked Policing:' A Reality in all Black Communities Throughout America." (blog) Ramona Houston, January 2, 2023, https://ramonahouston.com/social-impact-social-responsibility/wicked-policing-a-reality-in-all-black-communities-throughout-america/.

Hurd, Michael. *Thursday Night Lights*. Austin: University of Texas Press, 2017.

Jacobus, Robert D. *Black Man in the Huddle*. College Station: Texas A&M University Press, 2019.

Johnson, Rucker C. *Children of the Dream: Why School Integration Works*. New York: Basic Books, 2019.

Kellar, William Henry. *Make Haste Slowly: Moderates, Conservatives and School Desegregation in Houston*. College Station: Texas A&M University Press, 1999.

Ladino, Robyn Duff. *Desegregating Texas Schools*. Austin: University of Texas Press, 1996.

Lowery, Wesley. *They Can't Kill Us All*. New York: Little, Brown and Company, 2016.

Martin, Charles H. *Benching Jim Crow*. Urbana: University of Illinois Press, 2010.

McIntosh, K., E. Moss, R. Nunn, and J. Shambaugh, J. *Examining the Black-white Wealth Gap*. Washington, DC: Brooking Institutes, 2020.

McMurray, Bill. *Texas High School Football*. South Bend, IN: Icarus Press, 1985.

Myrdal, Gunnar. *An American Dilemma: The Negro Problem and Modern Democracy*. New York: McGraw-Hill, 1962.

National Advisory Commission on Civil Disorders, *Kerner Commission Report on the Causes, Events, and Aftermaths of the Civil Disorders of 1967*, US National Institute of Justice, 1968.

O'Brien, Michael. *Hesburgh: A Biography*. Washington, DC: Catholic University of America Press, 1998.

Orfield, Gary, and Erica Frankenberg. "Increasingly Segregated and Unequal School as Courts Reverse Policy." *Educational Administration Policy* 50, no. 5 (2014): 718–34.

Osofsky, Gilbert. *The Burden of Race: A Documentary History of Negro-White Relations in America*. New York: Harper and Row, 1967.

Parks, Rosa. "Cradle of the Confederacy Letters." Rosa Parks Collection, Library of Congress, Box 18, Folder 10, 1957.

Pennington, Richard. *Breaking the Ice: The Racial Integration of Southwest Conference Football*. Jefferson, NC: McFarland and Co. Inc., 1987.

Ratliff, Harold. *Autumn's Mightiest Legions: History of Texas Schoolboy Football*. Waco: Texian Press, 1963.

Reardon, S. F., and A. Owens. "60 years after Brown: Trends and Consequences of School Segregation." *Annual Review of Sociology* 40, no. 1 (2014): 199–218.

Semuals, Alana. "The Utter Inadequacy of America's Efforts to Desegregate School." *The Atlantic*, April 11, 2019.

Sherrod, Rick. *Texas High School Football Dynasties*. Charleston, SC: The History Press, 2013.

Smith, James P. and Finis R. Welch. *Closing the Gap: Forty Years of Economic Progress for Blacks*. Santa Monica, CA: The Rand Corporation, 1986.

Travis, J., B. Western, and F. S. Redburn. *The Growth of Incarceration in the United States: Exploring Causes and Consequences*. New York: National Academies Press, 2014.

Tygiel, Jules. *Baseball's Great Experiment: Jackie Robinson and his Legacy*. New York: Oxford University Press, 1983.

Wilkerson, I., *The Warmth of other Suns: The Epic Story of America's Great Migration*. London: Penguin UK, 2020.

Wolters, Raymond. *The Burden of Brown: Thirty Years of School Desegregation*. Knoxville: The University of Tennessee Press, 1984.

Woodward, C. Vann. *The Strange Career of Jim Crow*. New York: Oxford University Press, 1955.

Index